▶ **King Returns to Washington**

DOI: 10.1057/9781137589149.0001

Palgrave Studies in Cultural Heritage and Conflict

Series Editors: *Ihab Saloul, Rob van der Laarse, and Britt Baillie*

This book series explores the relationship between cultural heritage and conflict. The key themes of the series are the heritage and memory of war and conflict, contested heritage, and competing memories. The series editors seek books that analyze the dynamics of the past from the perspective of tangible and intangible remnants, spaces, and traces as well as heritage appropriations and restitutions, significations, musealizations and mediatizations in the present. Books in the series should address topics such as the politics of heritage and conflict, identity and trauma, mourning and reconciliation, nationalism and ethnicity, diaspora and intergenerational memories, painful heritage and terrorscapes, as well as the mediated re-enactments of conflicted pasts.

Dr. Ihab Saloul is assistant professor of cultural studies, and academic coordinator of *Heritage and Memory Studies* at University of Amsterdam. Saloul's interests include cultural memory and identity politics, narrative theory and visual analysis, conflict and trauma, Diaspora and migration as well as contemporary cultural thought in the Middle East.

Professor Rob van der Laarse is research director of the Amsterdam School for Heritage and Memory Studies (ASHMS) and Westerbork Professor of Heritage of Conflict and War at VU University Amsterdam. Van der Laarse's research focuses on (early) modern European elite and intellectual cultures, cultural landscape, heritage and identity politics, and the cultural roots and postwar memory of the Holocaust and other forms of mass violence.

Dr. Britt Baillie is a founding member of the Centre for Urban Conflict Studies at the University of Cambridge, and a research fellow at the University of Pretoria. Baillie's interests include the politicization of cultural heritage, heritage and the city, memory and identity, religion and conflict, theories of destruction, heritage as commons, contested heritage, and urban resistance.

Published by Palgrave Macmillan:

Social Memory and War Narratives: Transmitted Trauma Among Children of Vietnam War Veterans
Christina D. Weber

Narrating War in Peace: The Spanish Civil War in the Transition and Today
Katherine O. Stafford

The Lebanese Post-Civil War Novel: Memory, Trauma, and Capital
Felix Lang

King Returns to Washington: Explorations of Memory, Rhetoric, and Politics in the Martin Luther King, Jr. National Memorial
Jefferson Walker

DOI: 10.1057/9781137589149.0001

palgrave▶pivot

King Returns to Washington: Explorations of Memory, Rhetoric, and Politics in the Martin Luther King, Jr. National Memorial

Jefferson Walker

Assistant Professor of Communication,
Louisiana Tech University, USA

palgrave
macmillan

DOI: 10.1057/9781137589149.0001

KING RETURNS TO WASHINGTON
Copyright © Jefferson Walker, 2016.

First published in 2016 by
PALGRAVE MACMILLAN®
in the United States—a division of St. Martin's Press LLC,
175 Fifth Avenue, New York, NY 10010.

Where this book is distributed in the UK, Europe and the rest of the world,
this is by Palgrave Macmillan, a division of Macmillan Publishers Limited,
registered in England, company number 785998, of Houndmills,
Basingstoke, Hampshire RG21 6XS.

Palgrave Macmillan is the global academic imprint of the above companies
and has companies and representatives throughout the world.

Palgrave® and Macmillan® are registered trademarks in the United States,
the United Kingdom, Europe and other countries.

ISBN: 978–1–137–58915–6   EPUB
ISBN: 978–1–137–58914–9   PDF
ISBN: 978–1–137–59033–6   Hardback

Library of Congress Cataloging-in-Publication Data is available from the
Library of Congress.

A catalogue record of the book is available from the British Library.

First edition: 2016

www.palgrave.com/pivot

DOI: 10.1057/9781137589149

▶ *In loving memory of Joan Driver and
Elizabeth DeWeese Walker*

DOI: 10.1057/9781137589149.0001

Contents

DOI: 10.1057/9781137589149.0001

List of Figures

▶

DOI: 10.1057/9781137589149.0002

Acknowledgments

This book is the culmination of nearly four years of research related to the Martin Luther King Jr. National Memorial in Washington, DC. Much of that research was conducted under the direction of Jason Edward Black at the University of Alabama. Jason is a brother, friend, and mentor, and I am profoundly indebted to him for his guidance. I am also grateful to many other mentors who helped shape this book from its formative stages, including Beth S. Bennett, Meredith Bagley, Karla Gower, and Kari Frederickson. Other colleagues have offered advice and camaraderie throughout this process; among whom, I would like to express my appreciation to Sally Hardig, Sherry Ford, Ray Ozley, Tiffany Wang, Ruth Truss, Ray Harrison, Carol Mills, Ashley George, Mike and Natalie Devlin, Wendy Atkins-Sayre, Charles Tardy, Frankie Glennis, John Saunders, Brenda Heiman, Shane Puckett, Kevin and Lisa Merritt, and Don Kaczvinsky. I owe additional thanks to readers and respondents who reviewed various parts of the book for conferences sponsored by the National Communication Association, Southern States Communication Association, and Alabama Communication Association. The team at Palgrave Macmillan has also earned my heartfelt gratitude for supporting and strengthening my work.

Outside of academia, I have an amazing network of friends who have supported me throughout the completion of this book. While I cannot possibly mention them all, I would like to thank Jenna Bellamy, Stephen Billy, Matt Chance, Trent Friday, Drew Granthum, Michael

DOI: 10.1057/9781137589149.0003

and Brandi Hill, Joe and Mary Howard, Greg Lee, Richie Lisenby, Clark Maxwell, Keith Shoemaker, Melissa Stano, Chris Waites, and Trey West. These friends, along with others from Montevallo, Tuscaloosa, Hattiesburg, and Ruston, constantly bring joy and laughter into my life.

Finally, I am thankful for the opportunity to express my love and gratitude to my family. My parents, Tom and Betty Walker, have always been sources of encouragement, wisdom, inspiration, and love. My siblings, Matt Walker and Jane Walker Herndon, are two of my best friends and closest confidants. My grandmother, Faye Walker; grandfather, Marvin Driver; brother-in-law, Josh Herndon; and many aunts, uncles, and cousins have all been hugely positive and caring influences in my life. My late grandfather, Thomas Walker Sr., personified integrity and hard work. During the completion of this book, I lost my grandmother, Joan Driver, and my sister-in-law, Elizabeth DeWeese Walker. Both were incredible blessings in my life, and I will be always grateful for their love and encouragement.

DOI: 10.1057/9781137589149.0003

palgrave▶**pivot**

www.palgrave.com/pivot

1
Introduction

Abstract: *Chapter 1 traces the public memory of King from his death in 1968 to the present day, examining how his memory has been publicly appropriated for various, contrasting causes and how he has ultimately come to be viewed as a "national savior." The chapter briefly discusses other relevant national memory sites and commemorative occasions, including Atlanta's King Historic Site and the federally recognized MLK Day, before introducing the King Memorial as the primary space for remembering King at the national level. This chapter's approach underscores the significance of the memorial, while introducing themes related to King's memory that come into play throughout the book.*

Keywords: civil rights memory; commemorative rhetoric; King Memorial; public memory; Martin Luther King, Jr.

Walker, Jefferson. *King Returns to Washington: Explorations of Memory, Rhetoric, and Politics in the Martin Luther King, Jr. National Memorial*. New York: Palgrave Macmillan, 2016. DOI: 10.1057/9781137589149.0004.

Sitting at their kitchen table in 1983, George Sealey and his wife, Pauline, discussed the lack of memorials in the nation's capital that were dedicated to African Americans. Washington, DC, then a predominately Black city, boasted few Black memorials and monuments, while the National Mall claimed none. Sealey brought the issue to several of his Alpha Phi Alpha Fraternity brothers, who agreed to campaign for the creation of a memorial to Dr. Martin Luther King Jr. on the National Mall.[1] As an African American activist never elected to office who preached a philosophy of nonviolence, King would certainly stand out from the presidents and war heroes then honored on the Mall. Yet somehow King's inclusion seemed natural. By 1983, King had already been memorialized with monuments, buildings, and roads throughout the country and, in November of that year, President Ronald Reagan signed a bill into law making King's birthday a federal holiday.[2] Moreover, while the Mall had long honored national heroes from the past, King was instrumental in giving the space actual historical significance by leading the 1963 March on Washington and delivering his celebrated "I Have a Dream" speech on the steps of the Lincoln Memorial. King *belonged* on the National Mall.

What began as an idea at a kitchen table turned into a massive twenty-seven-plus-year effort by public servants, Alpha Phi Alpha, the King Estate, and numerous other individuals and organizations that ultimately resulted in the Martin Luther King Jr. National Memorial. The Memorial opened in 2011, purporting to be a "public sanctuary where future generations of Americans, regardless of race, religion, gender, ethnicity or sexual orientation, [could] come to honor the life and legacy of Dr. King."[3] Fittingly, the Mall's first memorial to an African American opened during the term of the nation's first African American president, Barack Obama. Speaking at the site's October 16, dedication ceremony, Obama proclaimed, "[T]his is a day that would not be denied. For this day, we celebrate Dr. Martin Luther King Jr's return to the National Mall."[4] Obama and other speakers at the event recognized the importance of the memorial as a now-permanent fixture on the National Mall, the country's "front yard."

Located at the northwest corner of the National Mall's Tidal Basin, the Memorial's design draws inspiration from a quotation from King's "Dream" speech: "Out of the mountain of despair, a stone of hope."[5] The Memorial presents a physical manifestation of this metaphor through its primary design elements: a "Stone of Hope," a large granite stone inscribed with the image of King, placed in front of the "Mountain of

DOI: 10.1057/9781137589149.0004

Despair," two stones that serve as the central entryway into the plaza (Figure 1.1). The "Stone of Hope" features King standing and facing away from the two parts of the "Mountain of Despair," with arms folded and eyes solemnly gazing across the Tidal Basin toward the Jefferson Memorial. On either side of the Memorial's main features are polished granite walls inscribed with quotations from several of King's writings and speeches (Figure 1.2).

Throughout its conception and construction, the Memorial received national attention and praise for its efforts in celebrating King's memory. However, not all of the Memorial's attention was positive, as the media reported numerous controversies surrounding its history and design. Some critics railed against the King Memorial for being "made in China," drawing attention to the statue's design by renowned Chinese sculptor Lei Yixin, its use of Chinese granite, and the employment of Chinese labor.[6] Others, notably including the late author and activist Maya Angelou, criticized the Memorial for paraphrasing a quotation from King in a way to make him sound "arrogant."[7] The site's dedication ceremony was not without its own controversies, as Obama and other speakers turned the occasion into somewhat of a political forum.[8]

FIGURE 1.1 *The "Stone of Hope" in front of the "Mountain of Despair"*

DOI: 10.1057/9781137589149.0004

FIGURE 1.2   *Inscription wall*

As the first memory site of its kind on the National Mall and, especially, as a site simultaneously levied with both praise and criticism, the King Memorial proves itself worthy of scholarly attention. Adding further significance to any project examining King's memory are the many educators, activists, and members of the media who lament the perceived lack of knowledge of King's life and accomplishments, especially among younger generations of Americans. For instance, Jasmyne Cannick, an African American community activist and columnist, says of younger generations, "They don't know what organization he founded, they don't know key lines of his speeches, they don't know when he was killed. I'm embarrassed and disappointed by this."[9] When asked about King's identity, many individuals might produce answers no deeper than that of fourteen-year-old Marcus Brown: "I know he said, 'I have a dream.'"[10] The ways that King's memory is constructed for such individuals remains a potentially relevant topic for historians, rhetoricians, and public memory scholars to address. The memory of King constructed and institutionalized at the national level by the National Parks Service (NPS) makes the King Memorial a singularly important subject.

DOI: 10.1057/9781137589149.0004

Moreover, some scholars mourn the depleted mythic construction of King as the transcendent "national savior."[11] As the nation celebrated the first Martin Luther King Jr. Federal Holiday (MLK Day), in 1987, historian and activist Vincent Gordon Harding wrote, "It appears as if the price for the first national holiday honoring a black man is the development of a massive case of national amnesia concerning who that black man really was."[12] Harding added that society placed King into "the relatively safe categories of 'civil rights leader,' 'great orator,' [and] harmless dreamer of black and white children on the hillside," while forgetting him as an evolving, embattled, and confrontational figure.[13] In King's case, as the memory of his universal messages of peace and equality have been celebrated, his more specific agendas, messages, and accomplishments have been forgotten.[14] By studying the King National Memorial, I am able to examine this trend, of celebrating the general to the detriment of the specific, at the national level.

Another closely related and equally troubling issue to scholars is the mythic narrative of King as the *only* central figure of the civil rights movement. Historian Keith D. Miller explains,

> This often-recited narrative locates the start of the racial struggle in 1955, when Rosa Parks's arrest in Montgomery launched King onto the national stage. Next, the narrative relates several largely non-King protests. Then, it reaches three peaks: the King-identified demonstrations and jailings in Birmingham in 1963; the King-identified March on Washington later in 1963, capped by his "I Have a Dream," speech; and the King-identified Selma-to-Montgomery March in 1965. Finally, the narrative proclaims the movement died in Memphis at the exact moment when King fell to an assassin's bullet in 1968.[15]

Numerous historians and other scholars have repeatedly challenged this narrative in recent decades, yet the myth persists in popular memory.[16]

Rhetorical critics have demonstrated the prevalence of this myth through a wealth of civil rights-related memory scholarship. King is the most frequently remembered leader of the civil rights movement and, at times, is its lone representative. He is memorialized at the places of his birth and death, in addition to museums, roads, and buildings scattered across the nation. In his study of Memphis, Tennessee's National Civil Rights Museum, Bernard Armada explains that memory sites tell us "who/what is central and who/what is peripheral; who/what we must remember and who/what it is okay to forget."[17] Memphis's museum, located at the Lorraine Motel where King was assassinated, places King

DOI: 10.1057/9781137589149.0004

at the center of the civil rights narrative by telling the story of his final days. Victoria Gallagher studies the King Center, located at King's birth site in Atlanta, Georgia, and suggests that the plethora of King-related memorials "attempt to apply King's values, beliefs, and practices to contemporary issues."[18] In another valuable contribution to memory scholarship, Beth Messner and Mark Vail discuss the approximately 700 roads named after King throughout the nation, which serve as present and functional sites of memory.[19] Armada, Gallagher, and Messner and Vail demonstrate that King's memory has been made partial, useful, and nearly inescapable.

The discrepancy between the public memory of and the historical account of King's role in the civil rights movement can best be explained by distinguishing memory from history. Historian David Thelen suggests historians are "concerned above all with the accuracy of a memory, with how correctly it describes what actually occurred at some point in the past."[20] Public Memory scholars Carole Blair, Greg Dickinson, and Brian Ott counter, "If history can be said to be judged by its adherence to protocols of evidence, we might say that public memory is assessed in terms of its effectivity."[21] Whereas historical accounts seek objectivity and accuracy, memories are partial and partisan. To be sure, as Gallagher asserts, many commemorative artifacts "might be said to have an educational function."[22] However, as Bruce Gronbeck posits, the primary goal of these artifacts is most often to cultivate "useful memor[ies] that an audience can find relevant to the present."[23] This is the core of memory studies: the understanding that commemorative artifacts are activated by and are responsive to contemporary issues. Commemorative artifacts offer stories from the past, morals included, that educate and build group identity. Commemorative artifacts justify positions, explain problems, and offer solutions. As cultural historian Michael Kammen suggests, "Societies... reconstruct their pasts rather than faithfully record them, and... they do so with needs of contemporary culture clearly in mind— manipulating the past in order to mold the present."[24]

A crucially important tenet of public memory is that it is material, textured, and, as historian Nathan Wachtel puts it, "anchor[ed] in space."[25] In his 1989 essay, "Between Memory and History," French historian Pierre Nora discusses *les lieux de mémoire*, or "sites of memory," asserting that "memory attaches itself to sites" and "takes root in the concrete, in spaces, gestures, images, and objects."[26] That is, physical sites of memory exist, such as cemeteries, churches, memorials, battlefields,

DOI: 10.1057/9781137589149.0004

monuments, museums, and homes. In the years since the publication of Nora's landmark essay, numerous scholars in rhetoric, history, art history, and cultural studies have taken up the study of memory sites under the umbrella of public, or collective, memory. Blair, Dickinson, and Ott describe the field of public memory as, "those studies taking the stance that beliefs about the past are shared among members of a group, whether a local community or the citizens of a nation-state."[27] Public memory scholars most often study memorials and museums, analyzing the sites' material and symbolic form and consequence.[28]

Scholars take a variety of approaches to critiquing sites of memory, most often engaging in some type of walk-through of the sites themselves and offering analysis concerning the sites' visual, textual, and other material and/or symbolic elements. Gallagher tells us that memory sites "may be examined in terms of form/style and content as are speeches and literary works."[29] However, Dickinson, Ott, and Eric Aoki explain that "traditional objects of rhetorical study such as public speeches have relatively clear beginnings and endings," making them very different from material artifacts.[30] Whereas speeches are "over," and books are "finished," material artifacts, including memory sites, call attention to their "presentness," existing as contemporary, ongoing pieces of rhetoric for as long as we observe them.[31] Most public memory scholars heed the presentness and ostensible permanence of memory sites, analyzing their form and function.

In addition to analyzing the sites themselves, many scholars recommend looking beyond the boundaries of memorials and museums to surrounding landscapes and to related texts. Dickinson, Ott, and Aoki reason, "historical and cultural sites are part of the texture of larger landscapes. The experience of museums and memorials does not begin at their entrances. Visitors must travel to these sites, which are often surrounded by other historical or tourist sites."[32] The authors suggest that critics attend to memory sites' landscapes (both physical and cognitive), as they might affect how audiences view and interpret the site. Adding to the list of what might impact memory-making at memorials, V. William Balthrop, Blair, and Neil Michel argue for studying dedication ceremonies as "supplemental rhetoric" to a site, asserting that "[r]itual dedications of commemorative sites are important not only as generic cultural initiations, but as interpretive apertures. The rhetoric of such events usually provides guidance to the audience, offering or implying interpretations of the site that are preferred by those empowered to offer them."[33] Commemorative rhetoric delivered at museums and memorials may influence how visitors come to view those sites. Rhetorical scholars Danielle Endres and Samantha Senda-Cook take this position a step further, adding that rhetoric delivered at places, including at memory sites, can "temporarily reconstruct the meaning (and challenge the dominant meaning) of a particular place" and can even "result in new place meanings."[34] Rhetorical readings of memory sites that do not take into account a site's surrounding landscape and various forms of "supplemental rhetoric" may be missing key fragments of the site's conglomerated whole.

When scholars take surrounding landscapes, interactions with other visitors, and related commemorative rhetoric into account, they may arrive at an inestimable number of interpretations. In addition, people interpret rhetorical texts including memory sites differently because of their own beliefs and experiences, in addition to demographic characteristics such as age, class, gender, race, religion, ability, and sexual orientation. Adding further complexity, communication scholars Victoria Sanchez and Mary Stuckey write,

> [E]ven as individual interpretations of a text are influenced by demographics and past experiences, the text itself contributes to experience. Just as images and stereotypes can be created and reinforced in texts, they can also be challenged, reformed, and remade during the process of reading or viewing.[35]

Rhetorical texts often contain complex, contradictory messages that can be interpreted as positive and negative, supportive and challenging, and in the words of Sanchez and Stuckey, "hegemonic and emancipatory."[36] Blair, Marsha Jeppeson, and Enrico Pucci Jr. label the rhetoric of such memorials as "multivocal."[37] That is, the sites hold multiple meanings that allow for—and encourage—different and even conflicting readings. Memory scholars must acknowledge that readings are imperfect and are in no way definitive or comprehensive of how all others might interpret a site.

Acknowledging individual readings as imperfect and in recognition of the ways that other rhetorical texts and contexts can play a role in constructing public memory, this book employs a multifaceted approach in its analysis of the King Memorial's form and function. This approach allows me to offer my own rhetorical analysis of the site, while also attending to how the Memorial's creators, benefactors, and observers have interpreted the site.

DOI: 10.1057/9781137589149.0004

Chapter 2 proceeds by exploring the conspicuous motives of the rhetors (as reflected and intimated in public discourse) behind the Memorial through a historical-contextual examination of the Memorial's conception, planning, and construction. By tracing the Memorial's history from its conception and approval to its design and construction, this chapter recovers the multivalent messages that the site's producers apparently sought to convey.

Recounting the Memorial's history also elucidates prominent critical and positive responses to the site, showing the variety of interpretations that have proliferated among its critics and supporters.

Chapter 3 presents my own critical interpretation of the King Memorial, assessing its rhetorical character and significance. Based primarily on my own encounter with the site (in situ), the chapter offers a composite reading of the site's textual composition and visual design. Additionally, this chapter attends to supplementary materials produced by the National Parks Service, including pamphlets and guidebooks distributed on-site and a free mobile phone app. By analyzing the site and its supplementary texts, I call attention to which memories are included in the site and which are forgotten or ignored. In the chapter, I also discuss the King Memorial's surrounding physical landscape (e.g., the National Mall and other nearby attractions) and cognitive landscape (e.g., the experiences and memories that visitors bring with them to the site) in order to demonstrate the ways in which traveling to the site impacts its rhetorical effect.

Chapter 4 offers a rhetorical analysis of the King Memorial's dedication ceremony, recognizing the occasion as a hegemonic vehicle for interpreting the site and underscoring the event's significance in influencing how others might also view the Memorial. The chapter argues that the ceremony functioned as a quasi-political forum that tied King's memory to many present-day events. Thus, the event not only presented the official or, at least, preferred interpretations of the site as articulated by those empowered to speak or perform but additionally linked King's memory to contemporary political issues. The chapter pays special attention to President Obama's remarks, arguing that Obama cultivated and used a memory of King in an effort to enhance his own personal ethos. Finally, the chapter examines how event participants helped the Memorial institutionalize King's memory.

Ultimately, this book offers a critical interpretation of the King Memorial and explores other interpretations in order to uncover how

DOI: 10.1057/9781137589149.0004

the site contributes to the public memory of Dr. Martin Luther King Jr. Through the critical interpretation of the Memorial and its related texts, the book addresses questions such as the following: How do the King Memorial's various components (e.g., location, textual features, visual elements, and experiential landscape) add contour to King's public memory? How might the memorial's visitors, critics, and producers arrive at different, sometimes conflicting interpretations of the site? How do related discursive texts (e.g., dedication speeches, pamphlets, articles, and editorials) influence the memorial's cultivation of King's public memory? In the end, this study contends that the King Memorial and its related discourse support different claims to "ownership" of King's memory. The book also asserts that the Memorial reconciles the memory of King and the civil rights movement with a "mainstream" narrative of progress throughout US history, institutionalizing King and transforming him from a vernacular voice to a hegemonic figure. Additionally, the book argues that the Memorial and its related discourse universalize King's memory, in the process turning the site into a contentious and contested rhetorical battleground. Chapter 5 summarizes the book's findings, expounding on these arguments and offering a robust and inclusive assessment of the Memorial.

Notes

1   Laurie Willis, "Long Road for MLK Memorial/It Started With a Couple's Conversation 17 Years Ago," *SFGate* (December 3, 2000), accessed January 13, 2013, http://www.sfgate.com/news/article/Long-Road-for-MLK-Memorial-It-started-with-a-2693246.php.
2   Ronald Reagan, "Remarks on Signing the Bill Making the Birthday of Martin Luther King, Jr., a National Holiday," *The American Presidency Project*, accessed January 9, 2015, http://www.presidency.ucsb.edu/ws/?pid=40708.
3   Harry E. Johnson, "The President's Letter," *BuildtheDream.org*, accessed September 9, 2012, http://www.mlkmemorial.org/site/c.hkIUL9MVJxE/b.1190535/k.5E36/The_Presidents_Letter.htm.
4   Barack Obama, dedicatory remarks at *Martin Luther King Memorial Dedication*, *C-SPAN* video, 3:22:36, Martin Luther King Jr. National Memorial, October 16, 2011, http://www.c-spanvideo.org/program/302020–1.
5   Martin Luther King Jr., "I Have a Dream," in *I Have a Dream: Writings and Speeches that Changed the World*, ed. James M. Washington (New York: HarperCollins, 1992), 105.

6 Paul Needham, "Martin Luther King Memorial: A 'Made in China' Design Comes to DC," *Huffington Post* (August 12, 2011), accessed September 9, 2012, http://www.huffingtonpost.com/2011/08/12/martin-luther-king-memorial_n_925341.html.

7 Gene Weingarten and Michael E. Ruane, "Maya Angelou Says King Memorial Inscription Makes Him Look 'Arrogant,'" *Washington Post* (August 30, 2011), accessed September 9, 2012, http://www.washingtonpost.com/local/maya-angelou-says-king-memorial-inscription-makes-him-look-arrogant/2011/08/30/gIQAlYChqJ_story.html. The memorial's inscription, "I was a drum major for justice, peace and righteousness," comes from a 1968 sermon in which King actually said, "If you want to say that I was a drum major, say that I was a drum major for justice. Say that I was a drum major for peace. Say that I was a drum major for righteousness. And all the other shallow things will not matter." Martin Luther King Jr., "The Drum Major Instinct," in *I Have a Dream: Writings and Speeches that Changed the World*, ed. James M. Washington (New York: HarperCollins, 1992), 191.

8 As I describe in greater detail in Chapter 4, these speakers discussed contemporary political issues including voting rights, education, immigration, and economic justice.

9 Jasmyne Cannick, as quoted in Daniel B. Wood, "Martin Luther King, Jr. and the Decline in What Younger Generations Know About Him," *Christian Science Monitor* (January 16, 2012): 1, accessed September 12, 2012, http://www.csmonitor.com/USA/2012/0116/Martin-Luther-King-Jr.-and-the-decline-in-what-younger-generations-know-about-him.

10 Marcus Brown, as quoted in Wood, "Martin Luther King, Jr.," 1.

11 Scott A. Sandage, "A Marble House Divided: The Lincoln Memorial, the Civil Rights Movement, and the Politics of Memory, 1939–1963," *Journal of American History* 80, no. 1 (1993): 166.

12 Vincent Gordon Harding, "Beyond Amnesia: Martin Luther King, Jr. and the Future of America," *Journal of American History* 74, no. 2 (1987): 469.

13 Ibid.

14 Throughout this study, I use variations of the words universal and universalize. I typically use universal as a descriptor before words such as values, ideals, and messages. By universal, I mean broad, abstract, and supposedly relatable to all or most people. I likewise use the word universalize to describe the action of making values, ideals, and messages broad, abstract, and relatable.

15 Keith D. Miller, "On Martin Luther King Jr. and the Landscape of Civil Rights Rhetoric," *Rhetoric and Public Affairs* 16, no. 1 (2013): 174.

16 For example, see Raymond Arsenault, *Freedom Riders: 1961 and the Struggle for Racial Justice* (New York: Oxford University Press, 2006); Charles Eagles, *The Prince of Defiance: James Meredith and the Integration of Ole Miss* (Chapel Hill:

DOI: 10.1057/9781137589149.0004

University of North Carolina Press, 2009); Cynthia Fleming, *Soon We Will Not Cry: The Liberation of Rudy Doris Smith Robinson* (Lanham, MD: Rowman and Littlefield, 1998); Davis W. Houck and David E. Dixon, eds., *Rhetoric, Women and the Civil Rights Movement, 1954–1965* (Jackson: University Press of Mississippi, 2009); Wesley Logan, *Many Minds, One Heart: SNCC's Dream for a New America* (Chapel Hill: University of North Carolina Press, 2009); Andrew Manis, *A Fire You Can't Put Out: The Civil Rights Life of Birmingham's Reverend Fred Shuttlesworth* (Tuscaloosa: University of Alabama Press, 1999); Kay Mills, *This Little Light of Mine: The Life of Fannie Lou Hamer* (Lexington: University Press of Kentucky, 2007); and Charles Payne, *I've Got the Light of Freedom: The Organizing Tradition and the Mississippi Freedom Struggle* (Berkeley: University of California Press, 1995).

17 Bernard J. Armada, "Memorial Agon: An Interpretive Tour of the National Civil Rights Museum," *Southern Communication Journal* 63, no. 3 (1998): 236.

18 Victoria J. Gallagher, "Remembering Together? Rhetorical Integration and the Case of the Martin Luther King, Jr. Memorial," *Southern Communication Journal* 60, no. 2 (1995): 111.

19 Beth A. Messner and Mark T. Vail, "A 'City at War': Commemorating Dr. Martin Luther King, Jr.," *Communication Studies* 60, no. 1 (2009): 17–31.

20 David Thelen, "Memory and American History," *Journal of American History* 74, no. 4 (1989): 1119.

21 Carole Blair, Greg Dickinson, and Brian L. Ott, "Introduction: Rhetoric/ Memory/Place," in *Places of Public Memory: The Rhetoric of Museums and Memorials*, ed. Greg Dickinson, Carole Blair, and Brian L. Ott (Tuscaloosa: University of Alabama Press, 2010), 9.

22 Victoria J. Gallagher, "Memory and Reconciliation in the Birmingham Civil Rights Institute," *Rhetoric and Public Affairs* 2, no. 2 (1999): 311.

23 Bruce E. Gronbeck, "The Rhetorics of the Past: History, Argument, and Collective Memory," in *Doing Rhetorical History: Concepts and Cases*, ed. K. J. Turner, (Tuscaloosa: University of Alabama Press, 1998), 57.

24 Michael Kammen, *Mystic Chords of Memory: The Transformation of Tradition in American Culture* (New York: Vintage Books, 1991), 3.

25 Nathan Wachtel, "Memory and History: Introduction," *History and Anthropology* 12, no. 2 (1986): 212.

26 Pierre Nora, "Between Memory and History: *Les Lieux de Mémorie*," *Representations* 26 (1989): 22, 9.

27 Blair, Dickinson, and Ott, "Introduction," 6.

28 For a sampling of rhetorical scholarship critiquing memory sites, see Jason Edward Black, "Memories of the Alabama Creek War, 1813–1814," *American Indian Quarterly* 33, no. 2 (2009): 200–29; Carole Blair, Marsha S. Jeppeson, and Enrico Pucci Jr., "Public Memorializing in Postmodernity: The Vietnam Veterans Memorial as Prototype," *Quarterly Journal of Speech* 77, no. 3 (1991):

DOI: 10.1057/9781137589149.0004

263–88; Carole Blair and Neil Michel, "Reproducing Civil Rights Tactics: The Rhetorical Performances of the Civil Rights Memorial," *Rhetoric Society Quarterly* 30, no. 2 (2000): 31–55; Greg Dickinson, Brian L. Ott, and Eric Aoki, "Memory and Myth at the Buffalo Bill Museum," *Western Journal of Communication* 69, no. 2 (2005): 85–108; Greg Dickinson, Brian L. Ott, and Eric Aoki, "Spaces of Remembering and Forgetting: The Reverent Eye/I at the Plains Indian Museum," *Communication and Critical/Cultural Studies* 3, no. 1 (2006): 27–47; Marouf Hasian Jr., "Remembering and Forgetting the 'Final Solution': A Rhetorical Pilgrimage through the U.S. Holocaust Memorial Museum," *Critical Studies in Media Communication* 21, no. 1 (2004): 64–92; Tamar Katriel, "Sites of Memory: Discourses of the Past in Israeli Pioneering Settlement Museums," *Quarterly Journal of Speech* 80 (1994): 1–20; Stephen A. King, "Memory, Mythmaking and Museums: Constructive Authenticity and the Primitive Blue Project," *Southern Communication Journal* 71, no. 3 (2006): 235–50; and Kenneth S. Zagacki and Victoria J. Gallagher, "Rhetoric and Materiality in the Museum Park at the North Carolina Museum of Art," *Quarterly Journal of Speech* 95, no. 2 (2009): 171–91.

29 Gallagher, "Memory and Reconciliation," 305.

30 Dickinson, Ott, and Aoki, "Spaces of Remembering and Forgetting," 29.

31 Gallagher, "Memory and Reconciliation," 305.

32 Dickinson, Ott, and Aoki, "Spaces of Remembering and Forgetting," 29.

33 William V. Balthrop, Carole Blair, and Neil Michel, "The Presence of the Present: Hijacking 'The Good War'?," *Western Journal of Communication* 74, no. 2 (2010): 171.

34 Danielle Endres and Samantha Senda-Cook, "Location Matters: The Rhetoric of Place in Protest," *Quarterly Journal of Speech* 97, no. 3 (2011): 259.

35 Victoria E. Sanchez and Mary E. Stuckey, "Coming of Age as a Culture? Emancipatory and Hegemonic Readings of *The Indian in the Cupboard*," *Western Journal of Communication* 64, no. 1 (2000): 78.

36 Ibid.

37 Blair, Jeppeson, and Pucci Jr., "Public Memorializing in Postmodernity," 264.

DOI: 10.1057/9781137589149.0004

2
"Building the Dream": The Making of the King Memorial

Abstract: *Chapter 2 offers a historical-contextual analysis of the King Memorial, collecting the publicly professed motives of the memorial's producers, along with the response from the site's critics and supporters. By tracing the King Memorial's history from its conception and approval to its design and construction, this chapter recovers the multivalent messages that the site's producers apparently sought to convey. By discussing the criticism and support that the project faced throughout its construction and upon its opening, the chapter also reveals public and vernacular interpretations of the site.*

Keywords: "Drum Major" quotation controversy; King Memorial; Lei Yixin; Memory Ownership; National Mall

Walker, Jefferson. *King Returns to Washington: Explorations of Memory, Rhetoric, and Politics in the Martin Luther King, Jr. National Memorial.* New York: Palgrave Macmillan, 2016. DOI: 10.1057/9781137589149.0005.

DOI: 10.1057/9781137589149.0005

In Rocky Mount, North Carolina, public outcry led to the 2005 removal of a statue of Dr. Martin Luther King Jr. Residents of the city, where King gave an early version of his "I Have a Dream" speech in 1962, complained that the statue bore little resemblance to King and compelled the City Council to take it down. What followed was an embarrassing turn of events, as a model of a proposed replacement statue was similarly rejected for its appearance, and the City Council returned the original statue to its place in the park only two years later. Dr. Elbert Lee, a civil rights activist who had protested the original statue, lamented its return, "To know a statue like that is going back up there, which will be there forever ... An unborn generation will never know the real appearance of Dr. Martin King." But City Council member Chris Miller said the statue "was intended to honor Dr. King and his life ... I was disappointed when it was taken down. Just differences of understanding, I think, about what a statue is."[1]

Controversies and "differences of understanding" with regard to memorializing King are certainly not unique to Rocky Mount. Also notable are efforts to remove the "World's Ugliest Statue of Martin Luther King" in Charlotte, North Carolina, and an eight-foot bust of King in Buffalo, New York.[2] Additionally, as Beth Messner and Mark Vail demonstrate, strife and controversy often surround the hundreds of the nation's streets named for King.[3] Unsurprisingly, then, the decades-long effort to memorialize King at the national level has encountered much disagreement and debate. This chapter recounts the history of the Martin Luther King Jr. National Memorial in Washington, DC, uncovering and interrogating issues related to its origins, location, design, and funding. This analysis pays special attention to the publicly discernible "intentions" of the Memorial's producers in order to clarify the messages they meant for the site to convey. This chapter also considers the positive and negative criticism levied at the Memorial in order to present vernacular interpretations of the site. This chapter contends that conflict and pragmatism compromised the various rhetors' desired effects of the Memorial. This chapter also argues that issues of memory "ownership" prevented a universally satisfying collaborative effort.

Origins

As Victoria Gallagher notes, before the King National Memorial came to fruition, only two other nationally based means of remembering King

DOI: 10.1057/9781137589149.0005

existed: the Martin Luther King Jr. Memorial Center in Atlanta, Georgia, and MLK Day in January. The Center was established with its first program in 1968, the year of King's assassination, although the Memorial itself did not open until 1977.[4] The establishment of a national holiday was a more complex affair, as Representative John Conyers of Michigan continually met resistance when introducing a bill proposing the holiday for fifteen straight legislative sessions beginning in 1968. President Ronald Reagan signed the bill declaring King's birthday a national holiday on November 2, 1983, and the country celebrated the first legal national holiday on January 20, 1986.[5]

Gallagher contends that these two national means differ substantially. She argues,

> The national holiday impinges on the lives of most, if not all, citizens by virtue of its inclusion on calendars and in school schedules. No matter what the quality, quantity, or social slant of one's memories of King, all citizens may be said to participate in the holiday in one way or another simply by living through the day.[6]

Meanwhile, the Center requires people to travel to a historic district featuring King's birth- and final resting places. While very different in form, the National Holiday and Atlanta's National Historic Site worked in conjunction with civil rights museums, regional memorials, and buildings and roads named for King in a common effort to spread his memory throughout the nation. But many people likely felt that King should also be remembered alongside other national heroes and icons on the National Mall in Washington, DC, which serves and has always served as the "public" space of reflection and repose in the nation's capital.

The twenty-seven-plus-year effort to bring the King Memorial to the National Mall began with a 1983 conversation between Alpha Phi Alpha Fraternity member George Sealey and his wife, Pauline, about the lack of memorials to African Americans in the nation's capital. Sealey and six of his fraternity brothers continued the conversation, focusing on King, who had been a fellow member of the nation's oldest African American Greek-letter fraternity. In January 1984, the group presented a formal proposal at the fraternity's Board of Director's meeting, and Alpha Phi Alpha soon began to champion the cause. But while Alpha Phi Alpha initiated and took charge of the project, fraternity brother John Carter insisted, "This is not an Alpha Phi Alpha memorial. It is not an African American memorial. This is a memorial for all Americans.

DOI: 10.1057/9781137589149.0005

Alpha is proud to be able to sponsor it, but it's gonna take all of America to build it."[7]

The Commemorative Works Act of 1986 prevents national memorials in the capital from honoring individuals until at least twenty-five years have passed since their deaths.[8] King's 1968 death meant that a memorial could not be approved or built until 1993 or later. The Senate first passed legislation to establish the memorial in 1991, but the twenty-five-year rule caused the bill to die in the House. The legislation finally passed both chambers with bipartisan support during the 104th Congress in 1996. Representatives Connie Morella of Maryland and Julian Dixon of California introduced the House legislation, which passed unanimously. Senators Paul Sarbanes of Maryland and John Warner of Virginia sponsored the bill in the Senate.[9] Sarbanes hoped the King Memorial would inspire the nation's youth. Voicing his aspirations from the Senate floor, he said,

> It is our hope that the young people who visit this monument will come to understand that it represents not only the enormous contribution of this great leader, but also two very basic principles necessary for the effective functioning of our society. The first is that change, even every [sic] fundamental change, is to be achieved through nonviolent means; that this is the path down which we should go as a nation in resolving some of our most difficult problems. The other basic principle is that the reconciliation of the races, the inclusion into the mainstream, of American Life of all its people, is essential to the fundamental health of our Nation.[10]

For Sarbanes, the Memorial would mean more for the future than for the past; it would encourage peace and civic engagement for future generations. President Bill Clinton signed the legislation on November 12, 1996, authorizing Alpha Phi Alpha to incorporate the Washington, DC Martin Luther King Jr. National Memorial Project Foundation (Foundation).[11] Headed by President Adrian L. Wallace and Vice President Carter, the Foundation began efforts to locate, design, and raise funds for the Memorial.[12]

Location

In June 1998, the Foundation gained congressional approval to locate the Memorial in Area 1 of the National Mall, the region where most of the prominent memorials stood, including the Lincoln, Jefferson,

DOI: 10.1057/9781137589149.0005

and Franklin Delano Roosevelt Memorials. This decision meant the Memorial would be the first to honor an African American on, or near, the National Mall. Carter testified before the Senate, adding that the Memorial also differed in another substantial way. Carter said, "We now have an opportunity to break the trend of memorials to war and erect a monument which delivers a message of lifelong peace in our land. A memorial which embodies not just the image of Dr. King, but the image of America, which is often called the melting pot of the world."[13] Carter saw the Memorial as a potential beacon for peace and diversity that would stand out from other monuments to war and to predominately white men who had served in politically high offices.

The Foundation examined several locations on the National Mall as potential sites for the Memorial and soon favored a four-acre site on the Tidal Basin. Two federal panels, the Commission of Fine Arts (CFA) and the National Capital Planning Commission (NCPC), had to approve the site by law. The CFA agreed to the Tidal Basin site, but the NCPC argued that the site should be closer to the Lincoln Memorial. Some wanted the Memorial in close proximity to the Lincoln Memorial to recall images of King's 1963 "Dream" speech. Others thought those memories could still be recalled in other areas where there would be more usable and flexible space for the Memorial. Behind the scenes, disagreements between the different parties were reportedly "emotional and divisive," as described by the *Spartanburg Herald-Journal*. "Each camp had a favored location and argued passionately about why the other sites were disrespectful to King's legacy."[14] NCPC Commissioner Margaret Vanderhye dismissed the Foundation's proposed site, saying, "Philosophically, it doesn't work. We can do better."[15] The NCPC rejected the Tidal Basin site in a seven-to-five vote on March 4, 1999, and instead recommended the east end of the Constitution Gardens, a location within sight of the Lincoln Memorial. Just over a month later, the CFA reviewed and unanimously rejected the NCPC recommendation and proposed two additional sites: an area on the west end of the Constitution Gardens and a place on the steps of the Lincoln Memorial.[16]

A memorial on the steps of the Lincoln Memorial would have undoubtedly recalled King's "I Have a Dream" speech during the 1963 March on Washington, as well as the event's connection to the one-hundred-year anniversary of Lincoln's Emancipation Proclamation. Such a memorial also could have radically changed the aesthetics and functionality of the Lincoln Memorial for various events. But some individuals, such

DOI: 10.1057/9781137589149.0005

as University of Pittsburgh History Professor Kirk Savage, favored the idea. Savage advocated for placing a statue of King in the spot where he stood to deliver his "Dream" speech, but acknowledged that his idea "would never happen." Instead, the NPS later placed a small plaque on the spot, in 2003, to commemorate the fortieth anniversary of the address.[17] Memorializing King at the Lincoln Memorial makes sense to a degree, but whether for practical, aesthetic, or other reasons, a full-scale monument at the feet of Lincoln never came to fruition. Perhaps such a memorial would have drawn criticism for only evoking the memory of King's most famous speech. Perhaps too the memorial would have been criticized for recalling the 1876 Washington, DC statue of Lincoln as the "Great Emancipator," with an African American on his knees, groveling at Lincoln's feet.[18] King, forever at the feet and in the shadow of Lincoln, or as historian and memory scholar Scott Sandage describes it, "King on those steps, reciting his Dream: Is this the new emancipation moment, at once liberating and limiting?"[19]

With a stalemate between the two federal commissions, NCPC Chair Harvey Gantt helped broker a deal resulting in a unanimous vote on December 2, 1999, to approve the original choice of the Tidal Basin site. Gantt commented, "Ultimately, it boiled down to the fact that nobody wanted to see an impasse on this ... Everyone wanted a memorial, and we had a heart-to-heart with members about how to make that happen."[20] The Foundation would later select 1964 Independence Avenue as the site's address, referencing the Civil Rights Act of 1964.

The chosen site was most noticeably adjacent to the Roosevelt Memorial, but the Foundation and the press were more eager to discuss its spatial relationship to the Lincoln and Jefferson Memorials. The Foundation described the location, across the Tidal Basin from the Jefferson Memorial and a short walk away from the Lincoln Memorial, as creating a visual "line of leadership" between the sites. Georgia Congressman and civil rights activist John Lewis said the site was "so fitting a tribute to Dr. King, his message and his legacy ... To have it between the Lincoln and the Jefferson, between the writer of the Declaration of Independence and the emancipator of the slaves." King's daughter Yolanda Denise King also spoke favorably on the location's proximity to the other memorials, exclaiming,

> I often say that George Washington birthed the country and certainly Jefferson was a part of that birthing. And then Lincoln was the one that allowed the country to move to the next level in terms of the unifying. And my father

DOI: 10.1057/9781137589149.0005

was the force that served to move us closer to actually being true to what was originally conceived on paper. So it is extremely significant.[21]

While some observers drew attention to Thomas Jefferson as a slave-holder, Lewis responded by saying, "[King] said that there would be a day when the sons and daughters of slaves and slaveholders would join hands together."[22] To Lewis and others, the relationship between the three sites had a reconciling effect.

Design

On February 15, 1999, the Foundation announced a design competition for the Memorial and disseminated information to architects, designers, and artists around the world. In December, the Foundation appointed a panel of 11 individuals from the fields of architecture, landscaping, and the fine arts to serve as competition assessors. By September 12, 2000, the panel had reviewed over 900 designs from fifty-two different countries and selected a design by ROMA Design Group of San Francisco, California.[23] The original design, largely consistent with the Memorial's final form, easily gained approval on April 18, 2002, from the CFA and on April 6, 2006, received acclaim from the NCPC for its "beauty and grandeur." Praise quickly turned into criticism, in 2007, when Chinese sculptor Lei Yixin joined the project as the head sculptor for the Memorial's primary design elements.[24]

Discovered by the Foundation at a 2006 Minnesota stone-carving symposium, Lei was best known for his government-commissioned sculptures of Chinese national figures such as Mao Zedong. The California chapter of the National Association for the Advancement of Colored People (NAACP) denounced the Foundation as "outsourc[ing] the production of the monument to Dr. King to the People's Republic of China, the country with the worst record of human rights violations and civil rights abuses in the world," adding that the sculptor was "renowned for his many sculptures and busts glorifying Mao Zedong, murderer of 70 million innocent Chinese, which is in direct opposition to Dr. King's philosophy and to the ideal of positive and social change throughout the world."[25] Many believed that the sculptor should be an American citizen, while some called specifically for an African American. Among them was Atlanta artist Gilbert Young, who launched the website www.kingisours.com to petition the Foundation to hire an African American sculptor.

DOI: 10.1057/9781137589149.0005

Young said, "It is disgraceful that there will be a sculpture to honor a black man for his fight against racism in this country and we couldn't find one black person on earth to interpret his likeness … It is insulting and does not serve my people well. It makes us invisible." Others agreed with Young in his assertion that "We need a black artist to interpret Dr. King … because he died for us." Foundation President and CEO Harry E. Johnson refuted such criticism by saying, "Dr. King was an international hero," and spoke practically, adding that "We searched the world looking for a sculptor who could do this work in granite and stone … There are no African American sculptors that do this type of work in granite."[26] Johnson further pushed back on criticism by emphasizing the involvement of two African Americans, painter Jon Onye Lockard and sculptor Ed Hamilton, who were collaborating with Lei.[27]

Lei's sculpture of King garnered disparagement in its own right. Lei covered his walls with pictures of King before beginning work on his first clay model featuring the civil rights leader, pen in hand, with folded arms. Explaining the goal of his design, Lei said, "When you see the statue of Martin Luther King, you might think of the injustices around the world, which call for our collaborative efforts … to bring to justice the things that King himself was unable to finish."[28] Lei's own description may explain the unfinished look of the King sculpture, as the sculptor insists that there is still work to be done in order to complete King's work. But criticism did not center on the sculpture's unfinished appearance. Instead, critics claimed the likeness of King looked detached, confrontational, angry, unreal, and/or "Asian."[29] American art and architecture scholar Michael Lewis writes that the most frequent claim against the sculpture was that "it recalls the despotic sculpture of Leninist-Maoist regimes, with their avuncular but stern 'dear leaders.'"[30] More plainly, frequent King sculptor Ed Dwight argued the statue design "didn't look like Martin Luther King. He had a whole bunch of wrinkles and great big bulky clothes. It wasn't right."[31]

For their part, the Foundation disagreed internally on the statue's design. They debated which of King's characteristics and values the sculpture should emphasize with its design. Lei said of the different views, "If there are 1,000 readers of *Hamlet*, you will have 1,000 [different] interpretations."[32] In April 2008, the CFA rejected the design, responding harshly that "the colossal scale and Social Realist style of the proposed sculpture recalls a genre of political sculpture that has recently been pulled down in other countries."[33] Within a month the

DOI: 10.1057/9781137589149.0005

Foundation, required by law to gain the commission's approval before proceeding, made minor changes in response to their criticism. These changes included smoothing away wrinkles from King's face and slightly reshaping his mouth, but did not address the major issues most critics complained about (e.g., the folded arms). Still, the CFA claimed their concerns had been sufficiently addressed and approved the design.[34] While many critics remained unappeased, key individuals behind the Memorial seemed content. King's son Martin Luther King III said, "I've seen probably 50 sculptures of my dad and I would say 47 of them are not good reflections ... This particular artist—he's done a good job."[35]

On Sunday July 22, 2007, Foundation President and CEO Harry Johnson accompanied Congressmen Lewis and Hank Johnson to Stone Mountain, Georgia, to inspect granite quarries for potential building materials for the Memorial.[36] This bold idea gained inspiration from King's reference to Stone Mountain in his "Dream" speech and from the location's complex and controversial history. Stone Mountain, a site associated with the South's "Lost Cause" memory and the 1915 rebirth of the Ku Klux Klan, hosts the world's largest work of sculpted art: a memorial to the Confederacy depicting Jefferson Davis, Robert E. Lee, and "Stonewall" Jackson. In 1958, the Georgia legislature voted to fund the Confederate memorial's completion, corresponding with their resistance to racial integration.[37] The use of granite from Stone Mountain could have enhanced the meaning of the King Memorial's central metaphor, as the "Stone of Hope" would have physically come from what was, to many people, a "Mountain of Despair."

Instead of stone from the controversial Stone Mountain, the Foundation eventually elected to build the Memorial's main features from Chinese shrimp pink granite. The Foundation anticipated criticism and defended their choice by claiming there was not a sufficient quantity of the granite in the United States. However, this did little to quell critics, who echoed their prior disapproval of the Chinese sculptor and blasted the choice. There were those who protested the use of Chinese granite and some who questioned the choice of a white-colored granite in the sculpture of a black man. Ed Jackson Jr., the executive architect of the King Memorial, explained that the white granite would look better to visitors coming at night.[38] As with the selection of the sculptor Lei Yixin, the decision to use white granite from China was, at least partially, a practical one, rather than something purposefully symbolic or meaningful.

DOI: 10.1057/9781137589149.0005

Unlike the design and construction of the "Stone of Hope" and "Mountain of Despair," which were fraught with controversy early on, the selection of quotations for the Memorial's walls was at first serene and largely uncontested. In late 2006, for the purpose of selecting quotations from King's sermons, speeches, and writings to be included in the Memorial, the Foundation assembled a council composed of historians and other scholars including Maya Angelou, Lerone Bennett, Clayborne Carson, James Chaffers, Henry Louis Gates Jr., Jon Onye Lockard, and Marianne Williamson.[39] The council set out to select quotations from different points in King's career that were "most representative [of] Dr. King's universal and timeless messages of Justice, Democracy, Hope and Love." The design team decided not to place the quotations chronologically in order to allow visitors to read the quotations as they liked, without having to follow a defined route. In total, the Council of Historians selected fourteen quotations for the Inscription Walls, the earliest from the Montgomery Bus Boycott in 1955 and the latest from King's final sermon at the National Cathedral in 1968.[40]

Noticeably and notably, the Foundation decided not to include any words from King's "I Have a Dream" speech on the Memorial's Inscription Walls. The Foundation listed several reasons for the omission: "Primarily, the entire memorial design is derived from King's most memorable speech; given the limited room for sharing his message and the breadth of his work, the overall design itself is the mark of respect for the moving words from 1963." The Foundation also reasoned that the "Dream" speech was King's best known and was already taught in schools. They explained, "But key messages that have and will continue to withstand the test of time are lesser known, and this memorial presented the opportunity to shift the focus of attention from one example of Dr. King's inspirational words to many."[41] With their selected quotations, the Foundation wanted to introduce visitors to King as a prolific wordsmith who crafted messages with universal themes.

While the Inscription Walls' quotations escaped controversy, a late change to the Stone of Hope's design created a large and lasting issue for the Memorial. The Foundation originally planned on placing two quotations on the stone: first, the site's only quotation from King's "I Have a Dream" speech, "Out of the mountain of despair, a stone of hope," and second, what Jackson Jr. called King's "own eulogy," "If you want to say that I was a drum major, say that I was a drum major for justice. Say that I was a drum major for peace. I was a drum major for righteousness. And

DOI: 10.1057/9781137589149.0005

all of the other shallow things will not matter." In a late decision, planners decided to change which sides of the stone each quotation would appear on, wanting the "stone of hope" inscription to be seen first by visitors entering through the Memorial's portal. Unfortunately, by the time they informed Lei Yixin, the sculptor had already prepared each side of the stone for their original inscriptions. The "drum major" quotation would not fit, and Jackson's design team faced a last-minute decision. Jackson said, "We sincerely felt passionate that the man's own eulogy should be expressed on the stone," and concluded "the least we could do was define who he was based on his perception of himself: 'I was a drum major for this, this, and this.'"[42] Thus, instead of selecting a new quotation for the spot, the designers decided to paraphrase King's quotation to "I was a drum major for justice, peace, and righteousness."

The most outspoken critic of the change was Angelou, who said,

> The quote makes Dr. Martin Luther King look like an arrogant twit. He was anything but that. He was far too profound a man for that four-letter word to apply. ... He had no arrogance at all. He had a humility that comes from deep inside. The "if" clause that is left out is salient. Leaving it out changes the meaning completely.[43]

In response, Jackson claimed that Angelou, who once served on the site's Council of Historians, failed to attend meetings at which the Memorial's quotations were selected. Jackson said that others on the council knew about and favored the idea of the paraphrased quotation and added that "I'm the guy that's making the decisions ... The buck has to stop somewhere. Otherwise we go round and round and round." Council member Jon Onye Lockard supported Jackson's decision, opining, "I think it's rather small of folks to pick at things. This has been going on for 14 years, and all of them have had plenty of time to add their thoughts and ideas."[44] Criticism seemed petty and unfair to many Foundation members, who had themselves argued over what others might identify as minor disagreements throughout the Memorial's conception and construction history. But Angelou did not stand alone in her criticism of the paraphrase. Others repeated the criticism of editorialist Rachel Manteuffel, who wrote that the quotation made King look like "arrogant jerk." She continued, "It's akin to memorializing Mahatma Gandhi with the quote, 'Don't you know who I *am*?' Even if the Mahatma said that once, it's not as though that is what we remember him for." But more important to Manteuffel was that the quotation was not exact. Offering

DOI: 10.1057/9781137589149.0005

another comparison she wrote, "This is the equivalent of a Hollywood publicist pulling four words out of context from a newspaper review to make a bad film seem good. Except in this case, it's the reverse: It takes the good out of context and makes it bad."[45] As the Memorial's dedication approached, this charge became the harshest and most widespread criticism that the site faced.

Fundraising

When asked how much the Memorial might cost, project originator Sealey initially guessed around $1.5 to $2 million, but by the time of its completion the total costs for the Memorial ended up being closer to $120 million.[46] The 1996 legislation authorizing the King Memorial stipulated that no federal dollars be used for the project, leaving fundraising duties to Alpha Phi Alpha Fraternity and the Foundation. Additionally, the legislation set a deadline of November 12, 2003, for the Foundation to raise $100 million for the project. By June of that year, the Foundation claimed $25 million in cash and pledges, and reported only $16,794 in money in the bank. Some criticized Alpha Phi Alpha for its handling of the fundraising. A *Village Voice* exposé described Foundation President Harry Johnson, who also served as the general president of Alpha Phi Alpha, as running the organization "as if it were purely an internal Alpha project" and recommended that the fraternity "look beyond themselves to make [the King Memorial] happen."[47]

On May 7, 2003, Senate Majority Leader William Frist hosted the launch of a national media campaign to raise funds for the Memorial.[48] The campaign, designed for free by Saatchi & Saatchi, featured television, radio, Internet, and print advertisements with celebrities including Halle Berry, Morgan Freeman, and Al Roker.[49] On August 28, Yahoo! featured the Memorial on its home page to help raise funds and awareness for the Foundation. However, the organization could not raise the money by their original deadline and had to seek an extension from Congress. Congress passed the necessary legislation on October 28, granting a three-year extension to Alpha Phi Alpha to raise the funds necessary for the Memorial.[50] The sponsors of the legislation reaffirmed their support for the project. Texas Congresswoman Sheila Jackson-Lee urged support for the extension, saying,

> [I]t is important in this time to give tribute to Dr. King on the basis of his call for peace and justice. He was a man who believed in nonviolent action, and

DOI: 10.1057/9781137589149.0005

he was a man who believed in peace over war and life over death. Now, in the backdrop of the violence of terrorism, but particularly in the predicament we find ourselves in Operation Iraqi Freedom, with our young men and women on the front lines and with a cry by the world for peace in the Middle East, it is important to honor Dr. Martin Luther King, a man of freedom, a man who promoted equality, a man of peace, a man who applauded and respected the diversity of this Nation.[51]

Jackson-Lee saw supporting the King Memorial as supporting the nation's professed values of peace, freedom, equality, and diversity. She also recognized the potential for King's memory to affect the nation's present circumstances.

With an extension granted, the Foundation continued its fundraising drive, attracting gifts from the public, in addition to corporate sponsors like Tommy Hilfiger, Walt Disney, State Farm Insurance, PepsiCo, ExxonMobil, BET, and Walmart.[52] Some critics, such as Syracuse University Professor Boyce Watkins, railed against the use of money from such donors. Watkins signaled out BET for "[creating] an entire generation of anti-intellectual Black youth and ... [for fueling] the Black HIV epidemic by promoting a lifestyle of sexual irresponsibility with non-stop booty-shaking videos." Watkins also targeted Walmart for its "long list of multi-billion dollar labor and human rights violations," and claimed that "If Dr. King were alive today, he'd be standing in front of Walmart with a picket sign, not asking them for money to build a statue."[53] By alleging foresight as to what a still-alive King would think and do, Watkins claimed moral superiority over the Foundation and its fundraising efforts. Other criticism of the fundraising process coincided with disdain for sculptor Lei Yixin. Some conspiracies held that the Foundation hired Lei in hopes of obtaining a large donation from the Chinese government. Johnson debunked such theories, repeating that the sculptor was hired for his expertise and experience.[54]

Adding to the Foundation's fundraising woes, the King family reportedly charged the organization over $800,000 for the use of King's words and likeness in fundraising materials. The King family, which owns King's intellectual property and likeness through the King Center and Intellectual Properties Management organizations, reached an arrangement with the Foundation that saw them collect $71,700 in 2003 and $761,160 in 2007.[55] Critics called the King family "shameless" and "greedy," but these were not new charges to King's children Dexter, Bernice, and Martin Luther King III. The King family had faced similar charges of

DOI: 10.1057/9781137589149.0005

dishonoring King's memory in the 1990s after successful lawsuits against *USA Today* and CBS for publishing the "I Have a Dream" speech without their permission.[56] King historian David Garrow was especially appalled and charged,

> I don't think the Jefferson family, the Lincoln family … I don't think any other group of family ancestors has been paid a licensing fee for a memorial in Washington. One would think any family would be so thrilled to have their forefather celebrated and memorialized in D.C. that it would never dawn on them to ask for a penny.

He added that King would have been "absolutely scandalized by the profiteering behavior of his children."[57]

Johnson insisted that the fees were not troublesome and maintained that the organization had a good relationship with the King family.[58] But some people behind the scenes, including a former executive director of the project, Paul Du Bois, described a different scenario. According to Du Bois, the King family initially asked that 50 percent of all money raised for the Memorial go to the King Center, which led Johnson to make a counteroffer of $600,000. Du Bois recalls Dexter King responding, "That's very generous of you, but my father was a spiritual man and he set aside the question of money, but if he were to take it—his spirit is speaking to me and he's saying it really should be $800,000." Johnson denied the allegation, and others have not confirmed Du Bois' report.[59] Johnson also assured critics that the Memorial's sculpture and the majority of its quotations were in the public domain, meaning that no further licensing fees would be charged. The King family told critics that they would not profit from the money, which would go to the King Center, adding that they worried fundraising efforts for the Memorial would lead to fewer donations for the site in Atlanta.[60] Regardless of its accuracy, the perception of tension and scandal did little to help fundraising efforts.

Fundraising materials often referred to the Memorial as the "Dream." The Foundation's website, www.buildthedream.org, alternately encouraged individuals to "Build," "Support," and "Become a 'Believer in the Dream.'"[61] A "Dream Team" of celebrities, such as Harrison Ford, Whoopi Goldberg, and Samuel L. Jackson, took part in "Dream Dinner" fundraisers throughout the nation. Likewise, a "Dream Concert" boasted Garth Brooks, Aretha Franklin, Carlos Santana, and other singers as celebrity participants. The Foundation's "Dream Keepers" College Program engaged students in fundraising efforts.[62] Conflating King's

DOI: 10.1057/9781137589149.0005

"Dream" trope from his most famous speech with the actualization of the Memorial, while understandable as a fundraising tactic, might have wrongly created the impression that the Memorial fulfilled King's "Dream." Watkins asserted that the "corporate memorial" might make King question the Foundation's understanding of his "Dream." He wrote,

> Dr. King fought for American equality in all areas that mattered, including education, economics, and incarceration, among others. As it stands, African Americans continue to be oppressed in ways that would make David Duke blush. Black children are not being educated, the wealth gap has grown to a level almost as high as when Dr. King was alive, Black unemployment is the highest that it's been in a quarter-century and there are more black men in prison than there were enslaved back in 1865. ... Whose dream is this?[63]

In spite of conflating the two as a fundraising strategy, the Foundation largely recognized the Memorial's completion as the fulfillment of its own dream, rather than King's. The Foundation described the finished site as a "living memorial," suggesting that the dream would not be completed but would live on at the site.[64]

Conclusion

Not unusually, tens of thousands gathered at the Lincoln Memorial on the anniversary of King's "I Have a Dream" speech in 2010, just over a year before the King Memorial's dedication ceremony. Surprisingly, though, the event was not a commemorative march or ceremony, but a rally to "restore honor in America" headlined by conservative media personality Glenn Beck and former Republican Vice Presidential nominee Sarah Palin. Beck called the rally a "moment, quite honestly, that I think we reclaim the civil rights movement," adding that "Whites don't own Abraham Lincoln [and] blacks don't own Martin Luther King."[65] The announcement of the event provoked a huge backlash, with some people claiming conservatives were "hijacking [King's] legacy."[66] Reverend Al Sharpton, a civil rights activist and politician, for instance, responded with a "Reclaim the Dream" rally in Washington on the same day to oppose Beck's event.[67]

This conclusion recounts the story of Beck's and Sharpton's opposing rallies to contextualize one of this chapter's central findings: the "ownership" of King's memory is often contested. In the case of the King

Memorial, that ownership dispute came in many forms. Gilbert Young claimed ownership on behalf of African Americans, declaring "King is ours" in protest of the employment of a Chinese sculptor. Others, such as Harry Johnson and Sarbanes, argued that King's memory truly belonged to African Americans, to all Americans, and perhaps to the entire international community. Alpha Phi Alpha Fraternity's involvement sometimes came into question, as critics pondered whether the organization was building the Memorial for its own benefit or for the nation's. Some feared that large corporate sponsors were trying to claim ownership of King's memory in moves to improve their own image. Finally, the King family's legal and economic rights to the slain leader's words and likeness caused critics to challenge their right to the ownership of his memory and their moral authority as stewards of his legacy. The larger question of ownership is at issue, or is, at least, reflected in each debate over the Memorial, from the conflicts over King's likeness and words to the disputes over location and funds. But as the clash over Beck's use or "hijacking" of King's memory demonstrates, the issue of ownership is not unique to this case study. Indeed, in 1986, the question of ownership arose with the creation of the federal holiday celebrating King's birthday. At the time, sophomore Republican Congressman Newt Gingrich asserted, "No one can claim Dr. King. He transcends all of us."[68] But was Gingrich right? Does King's memory belong to the few or to the many? To the past, present, or future? Chapters 3 and 4 present additional findings on the issue of ownership, and Chapter 5 further explores their implications.

This chapter's other central achievement was amassing the privileged motives behind and vernacular interpretations of the Memorial. The Foundation's creative urges and publicly meaningful purposes were sometimes tempered by practical concerns, as well as internal and external conflicts. For instance, primarily pragmatic reasons led the Foundation to use Chinese granite in constructing the Memorial's primary features, while time constraints and a lack of forethought led to the paraphrased "drum major" quotation. Conflicts over location and design also complicated open collaboration in some regards and forced various parties to compromise over the Memorial's final form. Ultimately, most public criticism during the Memorial's construction went ignored. But some affected change, including the "drum major" firestorm. On January 11, 2013, Secretary of the Interior Ken Salazar ordered that the paraphrased quotation be either eliminated or altered in response to

DOI: 10.1057/9781137589149.0005

continued criticism. The implication of such a change, as journalist Nick Carbone observes, is that "Some things aren't set in stone—even if they are set in stone."[69]

Notes

1   "Controversial MLK Statue to Return to Rocky Mount Park," *WRAL.com* (May 15, 2007), accessed January 12, 2013. http://www.wral.com/news/local/story/1417407/.

2   Shaila Dewan, "Larger Than Life, More to Fight Over," *New York Times* (May 18, 2008), accessed January 11, 2013, http://www.nytimes.com/2008/05/18/weekinreview/18dewan.html?_r=1&.

3   Messner and Vail, "A 'City at War,' " 17–31.

4   Gallagher, "Remembering Together," 110–14.

5   "History of the Memorial," *BuildtheDream.org*, accessed September 9, 2012, http://www.mlkmemorial.org/site/c.hkIUL9MVJxE/b.1190613/k.5EE9/History_of_the_Memorial.htm.

6   Gallagher, "Remembering Together," 110–11.

7   Laurie Willis, "Long Road for MLK Memorial/It Started with a Couple's Conversation 17 Years Ago," *SFGate* (December 3, 2000), accessed January 13, 2013, http://www.sfgate.com/news/article/Long-Road-for-MLK-Memorial-It-started-with-a-2693246.php.

8   Peter Grier, "Why MLK Memorial Is One of the Last New Structures on the National Mall," *Christian Science Monitor* (August 22, 2011), http://www.csmonitor.com/USA/DC-Decoder/Decoder-Wire/2011/0822/Why-MLK-Memorial-is-one-of-the-last-new-structures-on-the-National-Mall.

9   Rudi Williams, "Black Fraternity to Build D.C. King Memorial," *American Forces Press Service* (January 12, 1997), accessed January 13, 2013, http://www.defense.gov/News/NewsArticle.aspx?ID=43309. For examples of Memorial-related legislation and its related discussion, see 102 Cong. Rec. S15095, *THOMAS* (October 23, 1991), accessed February 14, 2013, http://thomas.loc.gov/cgi-bin/query/D?r102:56:./temp/~r102h8qIJx::; 103 Cong. Rec. E922, *THOMAS* (April 7, 1993), accessed February 14, 2013, http://thomas.loc.gov/cgi-bin/query/D?r103:1:./temp/~r103Fw4fvc::; 104 Cong. Rec. H11572, *THOMAS* (September 27, 1996), accessed February 14, 2013, http://thomas.loc.gov/cgi-bin/query/D?r104:1:./temp/~r104iX1dFJ::; and 104 Cong. Rec. S12439, *THOMAS* (October 21, 1996), accessed February 14, 2013, http://thomas.loc.gov/cgi-bin/query/D?r104:2:./temp/~r104YxQR7a::.

10 S. Rep. No. 104–190, *THOMAS* (February 15, 1995), accessed February 14, 2013, http://thomas.loc.gov/cgi-bin/cpquery/1?&sid=TSOPvtRpe&refer=&r_n=sr190.104&db_id=104&item=1&&w_p=king+memorial&attr=603&&si

DOI: 10.1057/9781137589149.0005

d=TSOPvtRpe&r_n=sr190.104&dbname=cp104&w_p=king+memorial&hd_count=7&item=1&&sel=TOC_2208&.

11 "History of the Memorial."

12 Willis, "Long Road for MLK Memorial."

13 "History of the Memorial."

14 Carol D. Leonnig, "Planners Pick Site for King Memorial," *Spartanburg Herald-Journal* (December 3, 1999), A3.

15 Associated Press, "Planners Reject Site for King Memorial," *Tuscaloosa News* (July 2, 1999), 1D.

16 "History of the Memorial."

17 Dewan, "Larger Than Life, More to Fight Over."

18 For a discussion on the statue, along with the history of African Americans appropriating the memory of Lincoln at the Lincoln Memorial, see Sandage, "A Marble House Divided."

19 Ibid., 166.

20 Leonnig, "Planners Pick Site for King Memorial," A3.

21 Molotsky, "Panel Approves Site for Dr. King Memorial."

22 Ibid.

23 Megan Gambino, "Building the Martin Luther King, Jr. National Memorial," *Smithsonian.com* (August 19, 2011), accessed January 12, 2013, http://www.smithsonianmag.com/history-archaeology/Building-the-Martin-Luther-King-Jr-National-Memorial.html?c=y&page=1.

24 "History of the Memorial."

25 Leslie Fulbright, "State NAACP Joins Protest of Chinese Artist Chosen for MLK Monument," *San Francisco Chronicle* (November 28, 2007), accessed January 11, 2013, http://www.sfgate.com/news/article/State-NAACP-joins-protest-of-Chinese-artist-3235257.php.

26 Ibid.

27 Ariana Eunjung Cha, "A King Statue 'Made in China'?," *Washington Post* (August 15, 2007), accessed January 11, 2013, http://www.washingtonpost.com/wp-dyn/content/article/2007/08/14/AR2007081401691_3.html.

28 Cha, "A King Statue 'Made in China'?"

29 Deron Dalton, "MLK Memorial Statue's Appearance Draws Criticism," *The Grio* (July 6, 2011), accessed January 11, 2013, http://thegrio.com/2011/07/06/mlks-memorial-statues-appearance-draws-criticism/.

30 Michael J. Lewis, "The Decline of American Monuments and Memorials," *Imprimis*, 41, no. 4 (2012): 7.

31 Cha, "A King Statue 'Made in China'?"

32 Ibid.

33 Dewan, "Larger Than Life, More to Fight Over."

34 Michael Birnbaum, "Arts Panel Members Satisfied with Changes to King Statue," *Washington Post* (June 20, 2008), accessed January 11, 2013,

DOI: 10.1057/9781137589149.0005

http://www.washingtonpost.com/wp-dyn/content/article/2008/06/19/
AR2008061902235.html.

35   Dalton, "MLK Memorial Statue's Appearance Draws Criticism."

36   "History of the Memorial."

37   David B. Freeman, *Carved in Stone: The History of Stone Mountain* (Macon,
GA: Mercer University Press, 1997), 2–3.

38   Clarence Page, "Give King Memorial a Chance," *Chicago Tribune* (August
28, 2011), accessed January 11, 2013, http://articles.chicagotribune.
com/2011–08-28/news/ct-oped-0828-page-20110828_1_lei-yixin-king-
memorial-project-martin-luther-king.

39   "Council of Historians Selects Martin Luther King, Jr. Quotations to Be
Engraved into Memorial," *BuildtheDream.org*, accessed September 8, 2012.
http://www.mlkmemorial.org/site/apps/nl/content2.asp?c=hkIUL9MVJxE&
b=1601407&ct=3560637.

40   "Design Elements," *BuildTheDream.org*, accessed September 8, 2012,
http://www.mlkmemorial.org/site/c.hkIUL9MVJxE/b.7548977/k.8C6B/
Design_Elements.htm.

41   "Design Elements."

42   Weingarten and Ruane, "Maya Angelou Says King Memorial Inscription
Makes Him Look 'Arrogant.' "

43   Ibid.

44   Ibid.

45   Rachel Manteuffel, "Martin Luther King a Drum Major? If You Say So,"
Washington Post (August 25, 2011), accessed January 15, 2013, http://www.
washingtonpost.com/opinions/martin-luther-king-a-drum-major-if-you-
say-so/2011/08/25/gIQAmmUkeJ_story.html.

46   Williams, "Black Fraternity to Build D.C. King Memorial;" Boyce Watkins,
"Five Questions Dr. King Might Ask about His Memorial Dedication
Ceremony," *Huffington Post* (October 19, 2011), accessed January 13, 2013,
http://www.huffingtonpost.com/dr-boyce-watkins/mlk-memorial-
dedication_b_1013945.html.

47   Thulani Davis, "Monumental Errors," *The Village Voice* (June 10, 2003),
accessed January 13, 2013, http://www.villagevoice.com/2003–06-10/news/
monumental-errors/.

48   "History of the Memorial."

49   Davis, "Monumental Errors."

50   "History of the Memorial."

51   108 Cong. Rec. H8422, *THOMAS* (September 23, 2003), accessed February 14,
2013, http://thomas.loc.gov/cgi-bin/query/D?r108:3:./temp/~r108pOJlig::.

52   "History of the Memorial."

53   Watkins, "Five Questions Dr. King Might Ask."

54   Cha, "A King Statue 'Made in China'?"

DOI: 10.1057/9781137589149.0005

55 Brett Zongker, "King Family Charges to Use His Words, Images," *SFGate* (April 18, 2009), accessed January 13, 2013, http://www.sfgate.com/default/ article/King-family-charges-to-use-his-words-images-3164227.php.

56 John Cook, "Martin Luther King Jr.'s Children Are Shameless, Greedy Shakedown Artists," *Gawker* (April 17, 2009), accessed January 13, 2013, http://gawker.com/5216918/martin-luther-king-jrs-children-are-shameless-greedy-shakedown-artists.

57 Zongker, "King Family Charges to Use His Words, Images."

58 Ibid.

59 Davis, "Monumental Errors."

60 Zongker, "King Family Charges to Use His Words, Images."

61 Harry E. Johnson, "Become a 'Believer in the Dream,'" *BuildtheDream.org*, accessed September 8, 2012, www.mlkmemorial.org/site/c.hkIUL9MVJxE/ b.1806459/k.155C/Become_a_Believer_in_the_Dream.htm.

62 "Programs and Events," *BuildtheDream.org*, accessed September 8, 2012, www.mlkmemorial.org/site/c.hkIUL9MVJxE/b.1215567/k.9A16/ Programs__Events.htm.

63 Watkins, "Five Questions Dr. King Might Ask."

64 "Mission & Vision," *BuildtheDream.org*, accessed September 8, 2012, www. mlkmemorial.org/site/c.hkIUL9MVJxE/b.1232927/k.9567/Mission__Vision. htm.

65 Richard Sisk, "Glenn Beck Rally on Anniversary of Martin Luther King Speech, Featuring Palin, Draws Ire of Sharpton," *New York Daily News* (August 26, 2010), accessed January 15, 2013, http://www.nydailynews.com/ news/national/glenn-beck-rally-anniversary-martin-luther-king-speech-featuring-palin-draws-ire-sharpton-article-1.200842.

66 Huma Kahn, "Glenn Beck's 'Restoring Honor' Rally Draws Tea Party Activists," *ABC News* (August 27, 2010), accessed January 15, 2013, http:// abcnews.go.com/print?id=11491130.

67 Sisk, "Glenn Beck Rally on Anniversary of Martin Luther King Speech."

68 As quoted in Sandage, "A Marble House Divided," 166.

69 Nick Carbone, "Martin Luther King Jr. Memorial 'Drum Major' Quotation to Be Corrected," *Time.com* (January 14, 2013), accessed January 15, 2013, http:// newsfeed.time.com/2012/01/14/martin-luther-king-jr-memorial-drum-major-quote-to-be-corrected/.

DOI: 10.1057/9781137589149.0005

3

The Rhetorical Form and Force of the King Memorial

Abstract: *Chapter 3 presents a critical interpretation of the King Memorial, assessing its rhetorical form and force. Based primarily on the author's own encounter with the site, the chapter offers a composite reading of the site's textual composition and visual design. Additionally, this chapter attends to supplementary materials produced by the National Parks Service including pamphlets and guidebooks distributed on-site and a free mobile phone app. By analyzing the site and its supplementary texts, I call attention to which memories are included in the site and which are forgotten or ignored. In the chapter, I also discuss the King Memorial's surrounding physical landscape (e.g., the National Mall and other nearby attractions) and cognitive landscape (e.g., the experiences and memories that visitors bring with them to the site) in order to demonstrate the ways in which traveling to the site impacts its rhetorical effect.*

Keywords: characteristics of public memorials; experiential landscape; fragmentary rhetoric; King Memorial; remembering and forgetting

Walker, Jefferson. *King Returns to Washington: Explorations of Memory, Rhetoric, and Politics in the Martin Luther King, Jr. National Memorial.* New York: Palgrave Macmillan, 2016. DOI: 10.1057/9781137589149.0006.

DOI: 10.1057/9781137589149.0006

This chapter offers a rhetorical analysis of the King Memorial based on two weekend-long visits in August 2012 and November 2013. I spent a majority of these research trips exploring the site, observing its visitors, talking to park rangers, and taking notes and photographs. This chapter's analysis is primarily based on my own observations, but also references the motives of the Memorial's creators and the critical response of the public. Additionally, this analysis attends to secondary sources produced by the NPS including pamphlets and guidebooks distributed on-site and a free mobile phone app.

Critical interpretations of commemorative sites can be problematic for a variety of reasons. The issue of authorship can be particularly murky, as collectives may collaborate, compromise, and compete over the particulars of a memorial. Explaining the significance of this issue, Blair, Jeppeson, and Pucci claim that "[n]o unity arises from collective design; in fact, plurality is cultivated. And authorial intent is of negligible value in interpreting a 'design' that may incorporate as many intentions as there are collaborative designers."[1] Therefore, this rhetorical analysis's foremost goal is not to evaluate the effectiveness of rhetors' attempts to imbue the Memorial with their intended messages. Instead, I heed commemoration scholars' insistence on "multivalent readings" and recognize the "goal is not to locate *the* message but the multiple, frequently conflicting messages."[2] This assertion of multivalence is consistent with one of the Foundation's professed views of the site: "This memorial is not designed to be experienced in a single way with one single message, but rather it is to have a broad accessibility, appealing to all of the senses with diverse and overlapping themes."[3] In this chapter, I recount multiple themes and interpretations pertinent to the Memorial, while also admitting that it is impossible to account for every theme the Memorial professes to include or interpretation that visitors may conceive.

Throughout this analysis, I initiate readings of the Memorial's visual and textual components, its surrounding landscape, and many of its supplementary materials, thereby taking a "fused approach" that analyzes "representative fragments of the site's milieu."[4] As rhetorical theorist Michael McGee says, using the concept of a "fragment,"

> emphasizes an important truth about discourse: *Discourse ceases to be what it is whenever parts of it are taken "out of context."* Failing to account for "context," or reducing "context" to one or two of its parts, means quite simply that one is no longer dealing with discourse as it appears in the world....Put another

DOI: 10.1057/9781137589149.0006

way, the elements of "context" are so important to the "text" that one cannot discover, or even discuss, the *meaning* of "text" without reference to them.[5]

Examining a representative sample of the site's many fragments ensures that the site is not taken out of its context and stripped of its meaning. Just as a reading of the site's visual elements would be incomplete without a reading of the site's textual components, a reading of the whole Memorial would be unfinished without a consideration of the site's many other fragmentary parts.[6] In whole, this chapter assesses the rhetorical form and force of the King Memorial not as a stand-alone artifact created by rhetors to cultivate memory in a certain way, but as an influential and complex text within an equally complex fragmentary landscape.

Based on its fragmentary nature within its surrounding landscape, I argue that the King Memorial institutionalizes and commodifies a memory of Martin Luther King Jr. that is partial and partisan. To expound upon this argument, I first discuss public memorials as fragmentary sites that serve educational and identity-building purposes. I next offer a brief descriptive walk-through of the King Memorial and its surrounding landscape. Third, I analyze the King Memorial and the ways in which it selectively remembers, institutionalizes, and commodifies an image of King. Finally, I conclude with reflections on what this analysis suggests about the functions of memorials and the state of King's memory.

The form and function of public memorials

Some scholars advocate what they deem to be the most crucial characteristics of public memorials. While these traits may be grouped together in various ways, in this section I condense what I have determined to be some of the most important consensual assumptions together into three multifaceted propositions: (1) memorials are purposeful, partisan, and partial; (2) memorials are part of larger physical and cognitive landscapes; and (3) memorials respond to present circumstances by educating and building identity.[7]

Memorials are purposeful, partisan, and partial

Blair, Jeppeson, and Pucci point out, "Public commemorative monuments...select from history those events, individuals, places, and ideas that will be sacralized by a culture or a polity."[8] Here, the authors note the consciousness and partiality of commemorative artifacts. As Nora argues, "there is no spontaneous memory," and "we must deliberately create archives, maintain anniversaries, organize celebrations, pronounce eulogies [and construct other types of commemorative artifacts]."[9] Rhetors mindfully decide on the *who, what,* and *how* of remembering. That is, they select items (the what or who) to remember and decide on how to remember them. Through this purposeful, partisan, and partial process of remembering, they also choose which details to minimize or forget.

Cicero recounts the story of the Athenian intellectual Themistocles, who confronted a teacher who offered to instruct him on the art of memory.[10] Themistocles responded by proclaiming he would rather learn how to forget, understanding that the "ability to forget what he did not want to remember was preferable to being able to remember whatever he had heard or just seen once." Although commemorative artifacts may attempt to forget, Cicero demonstrates the hardship of that goal. Blair, Dickinson, and Ott describe the remembering/forgetting dialectic as "nearly an assumptive cliché in public memory studies."[11] In rhetorician Bernard Armada's words, many scholars explore commemorative texts as they suggest "who/what is central and who/what is peripheral; who/what we must remember and who/what it is okay to forget."[12] Their purposeful and partisan nature always leads commemorative artifacts to selectively present fragments of the past. In addition, commemorative artifacts may be partial due to topical, financial, or time-related restraints, and "they can never present 'the' past in all of its social, cultural, and political complexity."[13] By leaving out content, rhetors establish what they deem to be most important for audiences to remember, but Blair, Dickinson, and Ott deny that the failure to represent content is a "sign of forgetting," instead calling it a "stand-in or simplistic restatement of the problem of representation."[14] A memorial that only highlights certain elements of a memory may not be purposefully trying to make audience members forget other related items. Additionally, that memorial is unlikely to succeed in making audience members completely forget other items, because no memory field is constituted by only one commemorative site or artifact. Indeed, although all memory artifacts are partial, audience members always view them within a context of other related memories.

DOI: 10.1057/9781137589149.0006

Memorials are part of larger physical and cognitive landscapes

Dickinson, Ott, and Aoki explain that all memory sites exist within experiential landscapes, which consist of surrounding *physical* landscapes
as well as *cognitive* landscapes. In a study of the Buffalo Bill Museum,
the authors explain the site's physical landscape, noting that visitors
must transverse through the Wyoming plains and also encounter other
memory sites, such as the Whitney Gallery of Western Art, the Plains
Indian Museum, the Cody Firearms Museum, and the Draper Museum
of Natural History. Moreover, the authors argue that the site's physical
landscape also includes nearby attractions such as Mount Rushmore, the
Crazy Horse Memorial, and other landmarks of the American West.[15]
Dickinson, Ott, and Aoki demonstrate that the surrounding physical
landscape affects a visitor's observance of a memory site. In essence,
the partial memory constructed by a commemorative artifact may be
supported, emphasized, challenged, weakened, mocked, or ridiculed by
its surrounding physical landscape.

Dickinson, Ott, and Aoki suggest that critics also examine the cognitive landscapes, or "dreamscapes," of commemorative sites. The authors
explain that the "experience of a particular place comprises not just the
tangible materials available in that place, but also the full range of memo-
rized images that persons bring with them."[16] In the authors' study of the
Plains Indian Museum (PIM), the site's cognitive landscape consists of
famous images of the West and representations of Native Americans. A
visitor to the site may remember Western films or "playing Indian" as
a child. Visitors to the PIM view the site as part of a larger cognitive
landscape, alongside their other related memories. As with the physical
landscapes, cognitive landscapes may alter the ways in which one reads
a memory text.

Together, the cognitive and physical landscapes surrounding spaces
of memory create what Dickinson, Ott, and Aoki call experiential
landscapes. These experiential landscapes "invite visitors to assume (to
occupy) particular subject positions. These subject positions, in turn,
literally shape perceptions, that is, they entail certain ways of looking and exclude others."[17] Communication scholar Marouf Hasian Jr.
examines the US Holocaust Memorial Museum (USHMM) as part of
an experiential landscape, with other famous memorials in Washington,
DC, making up its physical landscape, and visitors' other memories of

DOI: 10.1057/9781137589149.0006

the Holocaust and World War II making up its cognitive landscape. Hasian reports that the museum "allows audiences to bring their own experiences and prior knowledge to the museum," but "channel[s] [these experiences] into a discernible narrative."[18] As with other sites within their experiential landscapes, the USHMM promotes a subject position, encouraging visitors to perceive a topic in a certain way. Dickinson, Ott, and Aoki encourage rhetorical and cultural critics to be more attentive to the experiential landscapes of memory sites, advancing the idea that a site's "boundaries blend with the rest of the landscape, and the rest of the landscape is constituted, in part, by [the site]."[19]

Many scholars examine how the experiential landscapes of a commemorative artifact may alter an audience member's consumption of a public memory. Carole Blair and Neil Michel observe the Astronaut's Memorial in Cape Canaveral, Florida. The authors offer two readings of the monument, with the first presenting the place as a fitting memorial with the potential to engage audiences with the memory of the *Challenger* disaster.[20] However, Blair and Michel found that their initial reaction to the site was not shared by other visitors whom they observed. They observed that many visitors ignored the memorial, while others made only quick visits to the memorial and were hardly reflective. Through further observation and research, Blair and Michel discovered that a majority of visitors to the site all traveled forty miles from Walt Disney World. They were tourists in search of theme parks, rather than memorials. Additionally, the memorial itself was surrounded by the theme park of the Kennedy Space Center Visitor Center, also known as Spaceport USA. Blair and Michel's second interpretation of the site took this information into account, concluding that the memorial's surrounding landscape drastically changed the space's effect on audience members.[21]

Memorials respond to present circumstances by educating and building identity

Beyond their clear partiality and partisanship, rhetorical scholar Bruce Gronbeck posits that commemorative artifacts cultivate "useful memor[ies] that an audience can find relevant to the present."[22] Memorials and other commemorative sites respond to contemporary exigencies in ways that educate and build identity among audiences. Gallagher asserts that memory sites all "might be said to have an educational function,"[23] while Nora adds that we use such sites to "buttress our identities."[24]

DOI: 10.1057/9781137589149.0006

Gallagher clarifies that memory sites "differ both in the extent of the educational function and the need for it."[25] Some sites attempt to educate audience members on specific historical or cultural subjects, but many try to teach larger lessons on values and ideas. Dickinson, Ott, and Aoki view the Buffalo Bill Museum as a "pedagogical site, working to teach its visitors about the Old West and in so doing inculcating a particular vision not only of 'the West' but also of what it means to be American."[26] Gallagher examines the memory of Martin Luther King Jr. and suggests that the holiday, the memorial in Atlanta, and the numerous celebrations and programs "attempt to apply King's values, beliefs, and practices to contemporary issues."[27] These studies highlight the power of commemorative sites' abilities to educate the public.

Rhetorical theorist and critic Barbara Biesecker observes how commemorative artifacts of World War II, such as the film *Saving Private Ryan* and Tom Brokaw's book *The Greatest Generation*, "function rhetorically as civics lessons for a generation beset by factious disagreements about the viability of U.S. culture and identity."[28] Biesecker asserts that these texts remember the "greatest generation" in an effort to show modern-day audiences what it means to be a "good citizen."[29] Her essay operates under the "more or less explicit assumption what we remember and how we remember it can tell us something significant about who we are as a people now...and about who we may become."[30] The commemorative artifacts of World War II present a narrative of an actively engaged, patriotic community and encourage present-day citizens to follow in that community's footsteps. In a similar study that I have previously mentioned, Hasian argues that the USHMM is designed to "help with pluralistic lessons," allowing visitors to see "what happened when politicians and militarists abandoned the sacred tenets of civic Republicanism."[31] As do the other World War II artifacts examined by Biesecker, the USHMM venerates the traditional American values. In addition to educating the public on American values and the Holocaust, the site holds the potential "to play an active role in future policy and politics."[32] The site, along with politicians referencing it, may attempt to use the memory of the Holocaust "in the prevention of future genocides."[33]

In summary of these assumptions, memorials through their partial and partisan forms, existing within larger landscapes, and with the purpose of educating and cultivating identity are complex texts to analyze. Having delineated the form and function of public memorials, this chapter hereafter proceeds to examine the King Memorial. In the following pages, a descriptive account of the Memorial and its surrounding landscape precedes a thorough critical interpretation.

Descriptive analysis: the King Memorial and its experiential landscape

The Martin Luther King Jr. National Memorial stands on a four-acre site in West Potomac Park, a short walk away from the Lincoln Memorial where King delivered his iconic "I Have a Dream" speech in 1963. Of the many quotations inscribed on the Memorial's walls, only one comes from the "Dream" speech: "Out of the mountain of despair, a stone of hope" (Figure 3.1). This quotation serves as the Memorial's chief, inspiring metaphor, appearing on the side of the thirty-feet-tall, white granite "Stone of Hope," which also features the sculpted image of King. The quotation appears in the sight line of visitors entering through the Memorial's central passageway, composed of two other large slabs representing the "Mountain of Despair." The Memorial presents visitors with a physical and performative metaphor, as they themselves pass through the Mountain of Despair to arrive at the Stone of Hope.

Visitors must walk around the large Stone of Hope to its front side in order to view the sculpted image of King. The sculpture displays a full-body image of King in a suit and tie; he stands and gazes solemnly across the Tidal Basin toward the Jefferson Memorial. With his arms crossed, King clutches a scroll in his left hand, perhaps representing one of his famous speeches or written texts. Upon closer inspection of King's stern expression, visitors might notice that his eyes stare just to the right of the Jefferson Memorial, averting eye contact. King's figure is only partially carved from the white block of stone behind him that still encompasses his back and feet, giving the figure a purposely unfinished look (Figure 3.2).

On the Stone of Hope's side opposite to the "Mountain of Despair" quotation is a mostly blank wall. When the Memorial opened, this was the location of the controversially paraphrased quotation discussed in Chapters 1 and 2, "I was a drum major for justice, peace, and righteousness." This quotation was removed prior to the August 2013 celebrations of the fiftieth anniversary of the March on Washington. In its place are several horizontal "striation" marks, giving the surface a texture

DOI: 10.1057/9781137589149.0006

FIGURE 3.1   *The "Stone of Hope" inscription*

matching the rest of its rocky façade (Figure 3.3).[34] Sculptor Lei Yixin's signature remains inscribed in the bottom left corner.

Two long inscription walls stand on either side of the Memorial's entryway, quoting fourteen of King's best known speeches, sermons, and writings. A small water feature subsists where the inscription walls

DOI: 10.1057/9781137589149.0006

FIGURE 3.2   *King's sculpture in front of the "Mountain of Despair"*

meets the Mountain of Despair. Filling out the Memorial's plaza are several benches and plant life, including cherry blossom trees and crape myrtles. The cherry blossom trees surrounding the Tidal Basin origi-nated as a 1912 gift from Japan, signifying peace and unity between the nations. The NPS planted 182 additional cherry blossom trees around the

DOI: 10.1057/9781137589149.0006

FIGURE 3.3   *The blank wall where the "Drum Major" quotation was removed*

King Memorial, which only blossom for approximately two weeks every spring. The Foundation notes, "Poetically, each year the peak blooming period for the trees coincides with the anniversary of Dr. King's assassination, April 4th."[35] Other plant life, including the crape myrtles, offer prolonged blooming seasons and add to the site's ambience throughout the year. Meanwhile, American elm trees, the "standard street tree of Washington, DC," sit along the Memorial's border.[36] These trees serve to amalgamate the Memorial with its surrounding landscape, making the site fit in with the other monuments and landmarks around the city. Conveniently located across the street from the Memorial's entrance (and not visible from the site's central plaza) is a bookstore and ranger station.

The site's immediate surrounding physical landscape includes the National Mall, which primarily features monuments and memorials to various war veterans and presidents. From the Memorial, visitors can easily see the Washington Monument and the Jefferson Memorial. Meanwhile, the Franklin Delano Roosevelt Memorial is adjacent to the King Memorial, within a walking distance of one to three minutes. As discussed in Chapter 2, the Foundation is quick to highlight the

Memorial's place in a "line of leadership" with the Lincoln and Jefferson Memorials; a small information marker near the King Memorial also emphasizes this placement. Other notable memorials within walking distance include the Vietnam Veterans Memorial, the World War II Memorial, and the Korean War Veterans Memorial. While some visitors may come to the King Memorial for the express purpose of visiting the site, most will see the Memorial briefly as part of their trip's larger agenda. Additionally, residents of the city may pass by the Memorial on a stroll, run, or bike ride through the National Mall, as there is a popular trail that runs in front of the Memorial along the banks of the Tidal Basin.

The Memorial's greater physical landscape also includes the entire city of Washington, DC, home to a variety of important governmental, historical, and cultural landmarks. The city boasts a racially diverse population of over 600,000, with the majority being African American (50.7 percent), White (38.5 percent), or Hispanic (9.1 percent).[37] An additional 16 million visitors come to the nation's capital each year as tourists, businesspeople, students, activists, and in numerous other roles.[38]

Although Washington is racially, culturally, and ideologically diverse, and is generally thought of as open to a wide range of people, some view the city and the National Mall as inaccessible. Gallagher explains that the smaller number of African Americans honored by memorials in the city help make the capital and National Mall "more accessible to the experiences of white Americans."[39] While Gallagher's assertion is partly accurate, it draws attention to the city's changing physical and cognitive landscapes. Certainly many of the most noteworthy museums and memorials pay homage to white Americans; however, in the last twenty years, the National Museum of the American Indian, the African American Civil War Memorial Museum, and the United States Holocaust Memorial Museum have all opened, changing the outlook of whom the nation ought to pay tribute to. In addition, although the majority of landmarks in the nation's capital still celebrate the memories of predominately white Americans, many of these sites have been important historically to African Americans. Historian Scott Sandage traces the history of African Americans who demonstrated on the National Mall from a 1939 Easter concert to the 1963 March on Washington. The Lincoln Memorial, although not conceived for this purpose, became "racially contested ground" on which African Americans "strategically appropriated Lincoln's memory and monument as political weapons."[40] In all, the numerous museums and memorials, along with other historic

DOI: 10.1057/9781137589149.0006

sites, create a culture of commemoration in the city that encourages visitors and occupants to think about US history, culture, politics, and government. Steadily, these sites are encouraging visitors to consider culture and history that are not exclusively white and/or male centered.

The 2008 and 2012 presidential elections featured the most racially and ethnically diverse electorate in US history and saw the election of the nation's first African American president in Barack Obama.[41] Obama might be said to reside in both the physical and cognitive landscapes of the King Memorial. Obama has long recognized the link between himself and King, appropriating his words in many of his most important speeches.[42] On January 19, 2009, just one day before assuming the presidency, Obama celebrated MLK Day with a speech invoking King's memory from the Lincoln Memorial. As Obama literally walked in King's footsteps, the news media wondered aloud whether Obama, soon to be the first African American president, had symbolically fulfilled King's "Dream." Citing a CNN-Opinion Research Poll, political analyst Bill Schneider asked, "Has [King's] dream been fulfilled?... With the election of Barack Obama, two thirds of African-Americans believe it has."[43] The actual presence of Obama in Washington, DC, alters the physical landscape surrounding the King Memorial. Moreover, the presence of an African American president who called on King's words and potentially helped fulfill King's "dream" alters the cognitive landscape for those visiting the King Memorial, as individuals might have contemplated how King's legacy affected Obama and vice versa. An abundance of books written about Obama that are available in the Memorial's bookstore further place Obama's image and words within the King Memorial's landscape.

One final element to consider when describing the King Memorial's cognitive landscape is individual knowledge of King and the civil rights movement. Variations in prior knowledge can greatly impact the way one experiences the Memorial. As discussed in Chapter 1, actual knowledge of King's accomplishments is limited for many people. However, King's memory is celebrated throughout the nation in a variety of ways. Prior participation in MLK Day parades, school programs, and other events may affect how some view the Memorial. Other visitors may have lived through and experienced the civil rights movement firsthand. The diversity of knowledge and experiences among visitors to the King Memorial makes it impossible to predict exactly how each person will feel during his or her encounter with the site.

DOI: 10.1057/9781137589149.0006

A rhetorical analysis of the King Memorial

Having conveyed central characteristics of public memorials, along with a descriptive analysis of the King Memorial and its surrounding landscape, I turn now to a rhetorical analysis of the site. In the following pages, I examine the Memorial's tendencies to selectively remember certain parts of King's legacy, while concurrently institutionalizing and commodifying his image.

In cultivating a memory of King and the civil rights movement, the King Memorial performs certain pedagogical functions. Quotations from King's speeches and writings, in addition to information from park rangers help visitors understand more about King's life and philosophy. A plethora of books and other materials in the Memorial's bookstore offer an abundance of information for those wanting to learn about King and the civil rights movement. Yet in many ways, the Memorial privileges the present over the past and works to build identity rather than inform visitors about the historical King.

Obviously omitted from the site are images and words of other civil rights leaders. While their names appear in the books available for purchase and for some in the surrounding cognitive landscape, the Memorial itself makes no mention of other movement leaders. Furthermore, whereas the nearby Roosevelt Memorial depicts scenes from the Great Depression, such as men waiting in a bread line, the King Memorial fails to illustrate any of the hardships or triumphs of the civil rights movement. Instead, the Memorial presents only one image of King that is less than historically accurate. To begin, the sculpture honoring King is *white*, a design choice that might be said to downplay the importance of his race. Additionally, the King sculpture does not recall any specific moments from King's life. The image does not evoke King leading a demonstration as his legs and feet remain unfinished, engulfed in stone, rendering him unable to march. Nor does the image evoke King giving one of his famous speeches. King's lips are closed, his arms folded, and while he holds a scroll in his left hand, the document is blank and may not represent a particular speech or writing. Instead, the sculpture presents King as a philosopher, seemingly deep in thought.

The inscription walls quote fourteen speeches, sermons, and writings by King and, for the most part, continue to promote King as an abstract thinker. The majority of the quotations could be said to fit in the categories of "Justice, Peace and Righteousness," or love, nonviolence, and

DOI: 10.1057/9781137589149.0006

similarly general and universal descriptors. For example, the following inscriptions speak of largely universal ideals:

> We shall overcome because the arc of the moral universe is long, but it bends toward justice.—District of Columbia, 1968
>
> Darkness cannot drive out darkness, only light can do that. Hate cannot drive out hate, only love can do that.—1963
>
> Injustice anywhere is a threat to justice everywhere. We are caught in an inescapable network of mutuality, tied in a single garment of destiny. Whatever affects one directly, affects all indirectly.—Alabama, 1963

Whereas the Lincoln Memorial's interior includes the full texts of both the Gettysburg Address and Abraham Lincoln's Second Inaugural, the King Memorial's inscriptions are taken from a number of sources and presented with little context. The presence of whole texts, such as the 1963 "Letter from a Birmingham Jail," would likely discourage visitors from actually reading the inscriptions. Few would attend to the writings because of their length and the difficulty and awkwardness that might come from reading them from the walls. Instead of whole texts, then, the Memorial condenses King's words into bite-sized ideas. That is, as McGee observes, the reduction of an "apparently finished text into a fragment that seems more important than the whole from which it came."[44] The included quotations are placed in nonchronological, noncategorical order and offer only the year (and sometimes location) of their utterance or writing. The absence of additional context further demonstrates McGee's point that the fragment seems more important than the whole. Furthermore, the quotations are an apparent attempt to make King's words relevant and inspiring to a variety of present and future audiences. But absent of context and offering little about King's positions on the issues of his day, the inscription walls present King as an idealistic philosopher, rather than an activist who evolved in thought throughout his career.[45]

One quotation describing King's position on the Vietnam War is an exception to the universality and nonspecificity of the inscriptions:

> I oppose the war in Vietnam because I love America. I speak out against it not in anger but with anxiety and sorrow in my heart, and above all with a passionate desire to see our beloved country stand as the moral example of the world.—California, 1967

The Vietnam War quotation places King in time for visitors to the Memorial and also demonstrates his nonviolence agenda as more

DOI: 10.1057/9781137589149.0006

than a civil rights strategy. The quotation also can serve a purpose of identification for today's audience, as visitors might recall their own feelings on the Iraq War, the war in Afghanistan, or other present or future conflicts. The quotation reconciles patriotism with antiwar efforts. Two other more general quotations deal with war and nonviolence, as well:

> I believe that unarmed truth and unconditional love will have the final word in reality. This is why right, temporarily defeated, is stronger than evil triumphant.—Oslo, Norway, 1964.

> It is not enough to say "we must not wage war." It is necessary to love peace and sacrifice for it. We must concentrate not merely on the negative expulsion of war, but the positive affirmation of peace.—California, 1967.

The quotations on war and peace make this Memorial unique from the others on the Mall. Whereas the nearby monuments dedicated to veterans of World War II, the Korean War, and the Vietnam War commemorate the efforts of soldiers in combat, the King Memorial promotes peaceful protest. Whereas the presidential memorials all honor presidents who led the nation in times of war, the King Memorial commemorates a figure who supported nonviolence.

Another quotation gives an additional clue to its context, as some might recognize it from the Montgomery Bus Boycott, a landmark campaign in the civil rights movement.[46]

> We are determined here in Montgomery to work and fight until justice runs "down like water, and righteousness like a mighty stream."—Alabama, 1955

But while the quotation serves to recall a specific event for some, others might remain unaware of its more specific historical context. Indeed, the quotation primarily works as a call to action with the other more universal quotations including,

> The ultimate measure of a man is not where he stands in moments of convenience and comfort, but where he stands at times of challenge and controversy.—1963

> Make a career of humanity. Commit yourself to the noble struggle for equal rights. You will make a better person of yourself, a greater nation of your country, and a finer world to live in.—District of Columbia, 1959

Taken together, the quotations call on visitors to identify with King's seemingly universal values, rather than understand his complexities. Most of the quotations presented by the Memorial are relatively

DOI: 10.1057/9781137589149.0006

noncontroversial and abstract enough to apply to a host of present-day circumstances.

The removal of the paraphrased "Drum Major" quotation also serves as an example of the King Memorial promoting universal values over veracity. The paraphrased quotation, taken out of context, of course represented a disregard for the historical King. But the inscription's removal and replacement with what is essentially a blank canvas is also troubling. Rather than correcting the quotation or selecting another from King's many works, the Memorial sought to avoid further controversy and debate altogether. The erasure of King's words (although paraphrased) represents the Memorial's erasure of his more controversial positions. The now-blank wall represents the lack of information that the Memorial actually provides on King and the civil rights movement.

To this point, I have offered an interpretation arguing that the King Memorial strips King's image of his race, suppresses his ability to speak or move, and presents his words without context, thus cultivating a whitewashed image of King as an abstract thinker and philosopher. A more positive reading of the Memorial is possible, but still leads to similar conclusions. For example, visitors performing the site's central metaphor enter from the Mountain of Despair, representing the various hardships in their own lives to find promise at the Stone of Hope.[47] They may look at the King sculpture's blank scroll and incomplete rocky edges as symbolically representative of King's unfinished work, King's somber peering into the horizon as a reminder of the daunting journey still ahead. Such visitors return through the Mountain of Despair to apply King's values to their own lives. In the end, this interpretation still privileges cultivating identity and promoting engagement over educating the public about King's actual life and career. The Memorial's symbolic features also are vague enough to allow audiences to interpret what their specific identity is and what causes they ought to engage in.

Visitors looking for the historical King at the Memorial must look to the bookstore, in which they will find books, videos, and other materials focusing on King and the civil rights movement. Reflecting the Foundation's emphasis on educating younger generations, many of the books are aimed toward children. Among such books available during my trips were *Who Was Martin Luther King, Jr.?*, *The Civil Rights Movement for Kids*, *We March*, *Black Trivia: The African American Experience A-to-Z*, and a comic book titled *Martin Luther King, Jr.: Great Civil Rights Leader*. Other books and films focusing on King and specific movement events,

DOI: 10.1057/9781137589149.0006

such as the Montgomery Bus Boycott, are available for visitors who want deeper learning experiences.

While the bookstore performs pedagogically better than the actual Memorial, the bookstore also seeks to build identity and speak to present-day issues. During my first visit to the site, the table at the site's entrance displayed two books, a postcard, a keepsake box, an ornament, and a large flag with the image of King in front of the Stars and Stripes. While I first noticed the flag, I quickly turned my attention to the two books: *The Black Family Reunion Cookbook* and First Lady Michelle Obama's *American Grown: The Story of the White House Kitchen Garden and Gardens across America*. Although the shelves of the bookshop were lined with books on King and the civil rights movement, none were featured in the store's most prominent display. I soon learned that Obama's book was a new release and that the National Council of Negro Women's annual National Black Family Reunion was scheduled to take place not long after my visit on the National Mall.[48] However, the choice to display these books instead of biographies or history books demonstrates the priorities of the bookstore.

Elsewhere in the bookstore are several items exclusive to the King Memorial, including magnets, pins, postcards, bookmarks, posters, pencils, and ornaments. Most of these items feature pictures of King himself or of his image sculpted on the King Memorial. The bookstore thus uses King's image as a cipher, or a "basic figure and form for a variety of products and discourses within a much larger commodity field."[49] King's image helps market a variety of products to consumers, while also allowing them to take home fragments of the site to help in recalling their experiences with the Memorial. Images of the walls' inscriptions, along with copies of books, speeches, letters, and sermons written by King likewise enable visitors to take home pieces of the King Memorial in order to continue pondering King's legacy after they leave.

The bookstore also features items available at other locations on the National Mall, including books on presidents, NPS guidebooks, and maps of the area. Of particular significance to the King Memorial, although they were also available elsewhere, were books written about Barack Obama. As previously discussed, thoughts of Obama likely already proliferated through the minds of visitors to the King Memorial, as Obama and others linked his presidency to the memory of King. But the physical presence of Obama artifacts in the bookstore directly called on visitors to make a connection between the sitting president and King. Additionally, other contemporary presidents were included only in general trivia and history books marketed toward children. The bookstore most assuredly privileged the connection between Obama and King by packaging Obama artifacts alongside King's.

Conclusion and implications

This analysis affirms the following conclusions. First, while I have detailed what memories the King Memorial includes, I also recognize the significance of the site's ability to forget, ignore, "bracket out or elide" certain memories.[50] A comprehensive listing or description of every issue overlooked or discounted by the site would be inappropriate (and impossible), but I can attend to the Memorial's general omissions and speak to their importance. Notably, the site disregards other strands and leaders of the civil rights movement. Of course, the site is dedicated primarily to King, but it does not even speak to the conflictual or cooperative relationships between King and other notable figures such as Stokely Carmichael, Fred Shuttlesworth, or Malcolm X.[51] Such names might appear on the bookstore's shelves, but not in or among the most prominently displayed items. To use rhetorical scholar Philip Wander's term, some of these names might constitute a "Third Persona," or "the 'it' that is not present…a being whose presence, though relevant to what is said, is negated through silence."[52] But before passing judgment on all figures not explicitly named or depicted on the King Memorial as "negated," one must also recognize the site's limitations regarding which memories it can promote. Furthermore, I again acknowledge that public memory is constituted by the whole of a memory field and not by a sole memory site or artifact. Still, in consideration of these omissions, along with the site's lack of contextual information for each quotation and its privileging of noneducational memorabilia (e.g., Michelle Obama's gardening book), I can only conclude that the pedagogical goals of the Memorial take a backseat to other agendas. The Memorial's misquoted and mischaracterizing "drum major" inscription further supports the conclusion that issues of veracity and comprehensiveness are cast aside. Even in view of the larger experiential landscape of King's memory, an examination of the King Memorial does not answer the many concerns expressed in Chapter 1. Those lamenting the lack of knowledge of King's accomplishments find little reassurance in this site's rhetorical form.

DOI: 10.1057/9781137589149.0006

Of the memories included at the site, certain fragments are privileged over others. From the quotations selected for the inscription walls to the books displayed in the bookstore, the site promotes a distinct image of King and positive civic engagement. The general ambiguity of the Memorial's inscriptions allows visitors to easily identify with King's presented ideology and apply his words to a variety of positions. The lack of context and the shortage of more specific and perhaps controversial quotations yield an image of King as a nonpartisan, unifying figure. The site uses King's memory to promote relatively safe civic engagement by not specifying the issues or areas King might specifically engage in himself. The notable exception on the inscription walls is a quotation concerning the Vietnam War. In the climate of war, this quotation legitimizes antiwar positions and links them to patriotism. But even with that one quotation, the sum of the inscriptions offers a broadly appealing and very usable memory of King for visitors to take with them. The symbolic features also vaguely promote engagement, allowing would be activists to leave the Memorial and work for assorted causes under the auspices of King's memory.

Thus, the Memorial does little to quell the concerns of critics skeptical of the image of King as a universal hero. Vincent Gordon Harding's observation about MLK Day remains true in regard to the Memorial: the Memorial "had chosen, consciously or unconsciously, to allow King to become a convenient hero, to try and tailor him to the shape and mood of mainstream, liberal/moderate America."[53] By promoting King as a nonpartisan and uncontroversial hero, the Memorial risks misleadingly inspiring everyone or failing to inspire many. The Memorial forgets that King actually stood for specific issues. Failing to account for those issues threatens to leave hollow the hallowed ground of the Memorial.

The King Memorial develops an image of King as not only a unifying figure but also as a national hero. Adjacent to the FDR Memorial, in view of the Washington Monument, and in a "line of leadership" with memorials to Thomas Jefferson and Lincoln, King is situated among the most revered presidents in the nation's history. Alongside memorials to war veterans, King is honored with those who sacrificed life and limb in service of the nation. The Memorial's placement, grandeur, and even its landscaping allow visitors to see King as a key figure in the narrative of national progress. Certainly, positive implications come from King's move from vernacular to official within the national narrative. The shift in attitudes toward race and ideology should not go unnoticed.

DOI: 10.1057/9781137589149.0006

Additionally, King's legacy of peaceful protest joins war, depression, and political battle as part of the national struggle toward progress. But the move does not come without potentially negative consequences. Whereas George Washington, Lincoln, and the other presidents served the nation by executing laws, King worked to change policy. Whereas soldiers fought and died battling enemies from outside of the nation, King fought and died battling enemies from within. Does the Memorial legitimize the strategy of nonviolence by placing it next to the strategy of war? Or does it work the other way around? Does the placement of the King Memorial legitimize his views of the nation? Or does it silence his voice? The King Memorial's inscriptions, by inclusion and omission, say little on specific issues or the state of the nation. King's depiction is silent and still. The Stone of Hope carved from white granite also whitewashes many of the leader's beliefs. I return to these issues in the book's conclusion, but for now reiterate that consequences and tensions emerge from King's shift from a vernacular leader to an institutionalized symbol.

In the conclusion to Chapter 2, I discussed the contested "ownership" of King's memory. Here I add that the Memorial's textual and visual components indicate universal rights to his memory. Certainly, the image of King as a national hero supersedes any claims of ownership by individuals, races, or political parties. An included quotation might indicate King's own view on the issue:

> If we are to have peace on earth, our loyalties must become ecumenical rather than sectional. Our loyalties must transcend our race, our tribe, our class, and our nation; and this means we must develop a world perspective.—Georgia, 1967

Through its placement on the National Mall, the Memorial insists that King's memory belongs to the nation. By promoting the universal values of King, the Memorial insists that his memory also belongs to the entire world. However, self-aware of its surrounding experiential landscape, the Memorial subtly endorses one individual as the heir and steward of King's memory, if not its owner. Obama's physical presence at the Memorial (on the shelves of the bookstore), combined with his presence in the cognitive landscape of King's memory, bring him to the forefront of the "ownership" debate. As Chapter 4, discusses Obama's address at the Memorial's Dedication Ceremony, I leave further discussion of this issue for the remaining chapters of the book.

Finally, I return to this chapter's beginning assumption that memorials engender a plurality of readings. Alternative interpretations of the

DOI: 10.1057/9781137589149.0006

site are possible for those unhappy with King's depiction as cold and detached, or upset with a paraphrased quotation that mischaracterizes the slain leader. Also possible are readings of the site's central metaphor as positive and encouraging, inspiring individuals to strive for change. Others may view the site less as an inspiring memorial and more as a tourist destination. These individuals may engage with the site uncritically as a scheduled stop on their trip. Public memory then does not equate to universally consistent remembrances. Just as people come in with their own prior knowledge and expectations, they leave with their own interpretations and feelings.

Notes

1   Blair, Jeppeson, and Pucci, "Public Memorializing in Postmodernity," 270.
2   Ibid., 269. Emphasis in original.
3   "Composition and Space," *BuildtheDream.org*, accessed September 9, 2012, http://www.mlkmemorial.org/site/c.hkIUL9MVJxE/b.7548979/k.6200/Composition_and_Space.htm.
4   Black, "Memories of the Alabama Creek War, 1813–1814," 207.
5   Michael Calvin McGee, "Text, Context, and the Fragmentation of Contemporary Culture," *Western Journal of Speech Communication* 54, no. 3 (1990): 283. Emphasis in original.
6   Similarly, a reading of the National Mall as a larger "text" would be inadequate without considering each Memorial as a fragment.
7   This grouping of assumptions is partially based on the six characteristics of public memory advanced in Blair, Dickinson, and Ott, "Introduction," 6. The authors theorize that "(1) memory is activated by present concerns, issues, or anxieties; (2) memory narrates shared identities, constructing senses of communal belonging; (3) memory is animated by affect; (4) memory is partial, partisan, and thus often contested; (5) memory relies on material and/or symbolic supports; [and] (6) memory has a history." After reviewing the authors' list and surveying public memory literature, I determined the traits most significant to memorials in general and this case study specifically.
8   Blair, Jeppeson, and Pucci, "Public Memorializing in Postmodernity," 263.
9   Nora, "Between Memory and History," 12.
10 Cicero, *On the Ideal Orator (De Oratore)*, trans. James M. May and Jakob Wisse (New York: Oxford University Press, 2001), 2.299–2.300 (206).
11 Blair, Dickinson, and Ott, "Introduction," 18.
12 Armada, "Memorial Agon," 236.

DOI: 10.1057/9781137589149.0006

13 Ibid.

14 Blair, Dickinson, and Ott, "Introduction," 18.

15 Dickinson, Ott, and Aoki, "Memory and Myth at the Buffalo Bill Museum," 88.

16 Dickinson, Ott, and Aoki, "Spaces of Remembering and Forgetting," 30.

17 Ibid.

18 Hasian, "Remembering and Forgetting the 'Final Solution,'" 74.

19 Dickinson, Ott, and Aoki, "Spaces of Remembering and Forgetting," 41.

20 The *Challenger* disaster refers to the January 28, 1986, space shuttle accident that led to the deaths of seven crew members. Chris Bergin, "Remembering the Mistakes of Challenger," *NasaSpaceFlight.com* (January 28, 2007), accessed April 2, 2013, http://www.nasaspaceflight.com/2007/01/remembering-the-mistakes-of-challenger/.

21 Carole Blair and Neil Michel, "Commemorating in the Theme Park Zone: Reading the Astronauts Memorial," in *At the Intersection: Cultural Studies and Rhetorical Studies*, ed. Thomas Rosteck (New York: Guilford, 1999), 29–83.

22 Bruce E. Gronbeck, "The Rhetorics of the Past: History, Argument, and Collective Memory," in *Doing Rhetorical History: Concepts and Cases*, ed. K. J. Turner (Tuscaloosa: University of Alabama Press, 1998), 57.

23 Gallagher, "Memory and Reconciliation," 311.

24 Nora, "Between Memory and History," 12.

25 Gallagher, "Memory and Reconciliation," 311.

26 Dickinson, Ott, and Aoki, "Memory and Myth at the Buffalo Bill Museum," 88.

27 Gallagher, "Remembering Together," 111.

28 Barbara A. Biesecker, "Remembering World War II: The Rhetoric and Politics of National Commemoration at the Turn of the 21st Century," *Quarterly Journal of Speech* 88, no. 4 (2002): 394. See also Tom Brokaw, *The Greatest Generation* (New York: Random House, 2001); and *Saving Private Ryan*, directed by Steven Spielberg (Universal City, CA: DreamWorks SKG and Paramount Pictures, 1998).

29 Ibid.

30 Ibid., 406.

31 Hasian, "Remembering and Forgetting the 'Final Solution,'" 80.

32 Ibid., 85.

33 Ibid.

34 Brett Zongker, "Disputed Inscription Removed from MLK Memorial," *AP*, accessed February 6, 2015, http://bigstory.ap.org/article/disputed-inscription-removed-mlk-memorial.

35 "Design Elements."

36 Ibid.

37 "Quick Facts: Washington (City), District of Columbia," *United States Census Bureau*, accessed February 14, 2013, http://quickfacts.census.gov/qfd/states/11/1150000.html.

DOI: 10.1057/9781137589149.0006

38 "Media FAQs," *Washington.org*, accessed February 14, 2013, http://planning.
    washington.org/planning/press-room/contact-us/media-faqs#amtvisitors.
39 Gallagher, "Remembering Together," 116.
40 Sandage, "Marble House Divided," 143, 136.
41 Mark Hugo Lopez and Paul Taylor, "Dissecting the 2008 Electorate: Most
    Diverse in U.S. History," *Pew Research* (April 30, 2009), accessed February
    14, 2013, http://www.pewhispanic.org/2009/04/30/dissecting-the-2008-
    electorate-most-diverse-in-us-history/; Lydia Warren, "Record Number of
    Hispanic and Asian Voters Head to the Polls to Help Obama Secure Second
    Term—As His Support among Whites Plummets," *Daily Mail* (November
    7, 2012), accessed February 14, 2013, http://www.dailymail.co.uk/news/
    article-2229225/Presidential-election-2012-Record-number-Hispanic-voters-
    head-polls.html.
42 For example, see Barack Obama, "Pre-Inauguration Address at
    the Lincoln Memorial," January 18, 2009, transcript, *American
    Rhetoric*, http://www.americanrhetoric.com/speeches/barackobama/
    barackobamapreinaugurallincolnmemorial.htm; Barack Obama,
    "Nobel Prize for Peace Speech and Lecture," December 10, 2009,
    transcript, *American Rhetoric*, http://www.americanrhetoric.com/
    speeches/barackobama/barackobamanobelprizespeech.htm; and Barack
    Obama, "Second Presidential Inaugural Address," January 21, 2013,
    transcript, http://www.americanrhetoric.com/speeches/barackobama/
    barackobamasecondinauguraladdress.htm.
43 "Most Blacks Say MLK's Vision Fulfilled, Poll Finds," *CNNPolitics.com*
    (January 19, 2009), accessed October 16, 2012, http://www.cnn.com/2009/
    POLITICS/01/19/king.poll/index.html.
44 McGee, "Text, Context, and the Fragmentation of Contemporary Culture," 280.
45 The Inscriptions Pamphlet provides additional context for each quotation.
    For some quotations, the pamphlet gives a full citation. For others, the
    pamphlet briefly details the occasion for their utterance or writing. From my
    observations, few people picked up the piece of supplementary rhetoric.
46 Historian Peter B. Levy called Rosa Park's initial refusal to give up her seat
    the "shot…heard round the world" of the civil rights movement. The larger
    boycott captured national media attention and introduced King as a leader
    to many. Peter B. Levy, *The Civil Rights Movement* (Westport, CT: Greenwood
    Press, 1998), 9, 10–11.
47 I should add that while the Memorial's central metaphor makes sense for
    those entering through the Mountain of Despair, visitors may also enter from
    the walkway by the Tidal Basin. Those visitors, who may be coming from
    the neighboring FDR Memorial or from elsewhere, are unable to perform
    the metaphor perhaps as the designers would have it and instead instantly
    witness the Memorial's depiction of King, with the Mountain and inscription

DOI: 10.1057/9781137589149.0006

walls behind him. Such visitors also do not immediately read the quotation that inspired the Memorial, so for them the Memorial's metaphor may not be as apparent.

48   Dominique Browning, "Michelle Obama's 'American Grown,' and More," *New York Times* (June 1, 2012), http://www.nytimes.com/2012/06/03/books/review/michelle-obamas-american-grown-and-more.html?pagewanted=all&_r=0. The reunion was later canceled. Rachel Cooper, "Black Family Reunion 2012 in Washington, DC," *About.com*, accessed January 22, 2013, http://dc.about.com/od/specialevents/a/BlackFamilyReun.htm.

49   Kent A. Ono and Derek T. Buescher, "*Deciphering Pocahontas*: Unpackaging the Commodification of a Native American Woman," *Critical Studies in Media Communication* 18, no. 1 (2001): 24.

50   Hasian, "Remembering and Forgetting the 'Final Solution,'" 66.

51   I mention only three prominent names to indicate some of the most glaring omissions. I admittedly "forget" to include many movement leaders.

52   Philip Wander, "The Third Persona: An Ideological Turn in Rhetorical Theory," *Central States Speech Journal* 35, no. 4 (1984): 209–10.

53   Harding, "Beyond Amnesia," 468. I would add conservative, too, as only the most extreme would find nothing agreeable in the King Memorial's inscriptions or design.

4

Interpretation, Politicization, and Institutionalization: A Rhetorical Analysis of the King Memorial's Dedication Ceremony

▶

Abstract: *Chapter 4 outlines a rhetorical analysis of the King Memorial's dedication ceremony, which featured singers, celebrities, politicians, and activists, and culminated with a speech from President Barack Obama. Significantly, this chapter reveals the official or, at least, preferred interpretations of the site as articulated by those empowered to speak or perform at the event. Additionally, the chapter discusses how those individuals linked King's memory to their own political agendas. Finally, the analysis examines how event participants helped the Memorial institutionalize King's memory.*

Keywords: King Memorial; Obama and King; Politicizing King's Memory; Institutionalizing King's Memory

Walker, Jefferson. *King Returns to Washington: Explorations of Memory, Rhetoric, and Politics in the Martin Luther King, Jr. National Memorial.* New York: Palgrave Macmillan, 2016. DOI: 10.1057/9781137589149.0007.

Originally scheduled for August 28, 2011, to mark the anniversary of King's 1963 "I Have a Dream" speech, the Memorial's dedication ceremony was delayed by a pair of natural disasters. First, earthquake damage caused organizers to change the locations of prededication festivities, moving a Wednesday night gala dinner from the National Building Museum to the Washington Convention Center, and a Saturday interfaith service from the Washington National Cathedral to the Basilica of the National Shrine. Next, the approach of Category 4 Hurricane Irene led organizers to post-pone the event entirely. Eventually rescheduled for Sunday, October 16, the Memorial's dedication took place under clear skies and moderate tempera-tures, and in front of tens of thousands of people gathered on the National Mall.[1] Several of the event's twenty-eight speakers noted the ceremony's delay in their remarks, including the headline speaker President Barack Obama, who began his speech, "An earthquake and a hurricane may have delayed this day, but this is a day that would not be denied."[2]

As Balthrop, Blair, and Michel assert, "Ritual dedications of commemo-rative sites are important not only as generic cultural initiations, but as interpretive apertures."[3] In other words, the rhetoric of a dedicatory speech or performance may influence how an audience member interprets a commemorative site. Unsurprisingly, in the case of the King Memorial, a number of the dedication ceremony's speakers offered guidance for interpreting the Memorial or, at least, offered their espoused goals and hopes for the Memorial's future. Among such speakers was King's sister Christine King Farris, who spoke of one general hope for the site, namely that it would "provide a source of inspiration for people all over the world for generations to come."[4] Other speakers also picked up on this motif, a theme I previously discussed as advanced by the King Memorial itself and the voices of its creators. But while the speakers praised the site as "the world's memorial" (Foundation president and CEO Harry Johnson), they concurrently and conversely also cultivated very partisan and political memories of King himself.[5] The dedicators linked King's public memory to contemporary issues as diverse as education, economic justice, and Lesbian, Gay, Bisexual, Transgender, and Queer (LGBTQ) rights. Although inconsistent with their presentation of the King Memorial as a universally appealing site, the cultivation of usable, political memories of King was consistent with the central scholarly assumptions of public memory as intentional, partisan, partial, and present focused.

This chapter examines the dedication ceremony not only as a celebra-tory event but also as a sort of political forum. I divide my analysis into

DOI: 10.1057/9781137589149.0007

three parts. First, I elucidate event participants' most overt interpretations of the Memorial and its goals, contending that the somewhat exclusive group of interpreters generally read the site as unifying and inspiring. Second, I examine the speakers' efforts to cultivate a political memory of King, arguing that while most speakers drastically turned from their universal interpretations toward more partisan rhetoric, Obama actually avoided such a shift in order to maintain a usable memory for his own purposes. Third, I consider the event's varied efforts to institutionalize the memory of King, arguing that event participants attempted to place his memory within a larger mainstream national narrative. Throughout each section and in the conclusion, I observe the mounting tensions that arose from the event's melding together of the celebratory and the political, the epideictic and the deliberative, the universal and the partisan, and the official and the vernacular. I argue that event participants cultivated, used, and ultimately institutionalized a very political public memory of King.

Interpretation

In their most overt interpretations of the Memorial and its goals, speakers most often offered universal messages.[6] They repeated that they hoped King's memory could inspire people around the world and generally agreed that the Memorial meant as much to the present and future as it did to the past. In this section, I call attention to these universal interpretations, but also examine one notable deviation from the norm. Before discussing the interpretations offered at the event, it is insightful to review the list of participants itself.

The in/exclusionary participants

Just as the Memorial remembers and omits certain players from the civil rights movement, the dedication ceremony included and excluded participants whom one might expect to find at the event. Among the principle speakers were Master of Ceremonies Gwen Ifill (news anchor), Vincent Gray (mayor of Washington, D.C.), Julian Bond (social activist and professor), Christine King Farris (King's older sister), Reverend Bernice King (King's daughter), Martin Luther King III (King's son), Dan Rather (former news anchor and correspondent), Reverend Jesse Jackson (a fellow activist with King and politician), Representative John

DOI: 10.1057/9781137589149.0007

Lewis (a fellow activist with King and current elected official), Andrew Young (activist and former ambassador to the United Nations), Reverend Joseph Lowery (Southern Christian Leadership Conference cofounder), Reverend Al Sharpton (activist and politician), Marian Wright Edelmen (children's rights activist), Ken Salazar (secretary of the interior), Harry Johnson (Foundation president and CEO), and President Obama.[7] A glance at the list of speakers reveals notable politicians and public servants, celebrities, members of the King family, and activists who marched with and/or were inspired by King. While the principal speakers were mostly African American, several white speakers gave the occasion some semblance of racial variety. The speakers were also somewhat diverse in age, with the youngest being the twelve-year-old actor Amandla Stenberg and the oldest being the ninety-year old Lowery.

The speakers seemed appropriate enough for the occasion, and many of their absences would have been apparent had they not participated. But many groups were noticeably absent or underrepresented at the event. After all, dedicators interpreted the site as "[not just] for African Americans, but for Americans and citizens around this world" (Bernice King).[8] Yet only Americans spoke at the event. Bond remarked briefly on behalf of Yemeni 2011 Nobel Peace Prize recipient Tawakkul Karman, discussing the ways in which King's message "[resonated] in far away Yemen and everywhere around the world," but no foreign leaders or activists spoke for themselves.[9] The Israeli-born American violinist Miri Ben-Ari, the only event participant born outside of the country, did not have a speaking role at the event.[10] Furthermore, the event's dedicators were a somewhat racially and politically exclusive group, as only African Americans and white Americans who were primarily affiliated with the political Left delivered remarks.[11] The lack of racial diversity (beyond black and white) detracted from the Memorial's professed goal of inclusiveness, but more importantly the lack of diversity may have also limited the kind of interpretations offered at the event. Certainly, critics of the site's architecture, design, placement, and/or content did not speak out with their own interpretations at the event.[12]

Universal or confrontational?

Many speakers only offered their interpretations of the Memorial's general goals, including Lowery, who said, "While the presence of this imposing structure forever reminds us of the long and perilous journey that the struggle has brought us through, it also points towards the

DOI: 10.1057/9781137589149.0007

future."[13] Lowery's message reflected the interpretation that the sculpture of King was gazing across the Tidal Basin toward future struggles and successes. Bernice King similarly hoped people visiting the Memorial "could be propelled into action, utilizing [King's] philosophies and strategies of non-violence."[14] These speakers presented purposefully vague present and future-oriented goals for the Memorial. Such remarks were congruous with Johnson's view of the site as the "world's memorial."

Sharpton's and Obama's interpretations of the King Memorial's sculpture also urged action while remaining relatively uncontroversial. Sharpton called the sculpture "[a] man standing in a posture of faith," thus disagreeing with the vocal critics who derided the statue as aloof or confrontational.[15] Obama picked up on Sharpton's emphasis on faith when describing his primary hope for the site:

> In the end, that's what I hope my daughters take away from this monument. I want them to come away from here with a faith in what they can accomplish when they are determined and working for a righteous cause. I want them to come away from here with a faith in other people and a faith in a benevolent God. This sculpture, massive and iconic as it is, will remind them of Dr. King's strength.[16]

Obama's description of what his daughters might gain from the site echoed Bernice King's and Lowery's interpretation of the Memorial's potential to inspire and engage future generations. By focusing on "faith" and "strength," along with the unspecified "righteous cause," Obama crafted an abstract, unifying message.

But while Obama and Sharpton sought to avert controversy with their interpretations of the statue, Jackson apparently welcomed it. Jackson openly agreed with critics who voiced their opinions that the King sculpture appeared confrontational. However, unlike those critics, Jackson maintained that the figure's confrontational posture was a positive feature of the monument. Jackson said, "The image of a confrontational King may not be pleasing to those who seek to wash the blood stains from history but is useful to those who value the truth of King's life more than the myth of the man."[17] Jackson risked alienating portions of his audience who thought differently about the statue's posture, but to him the confrontational image represented the historically accurate King, as well as, in his own words, the most "useful" King. Jackson yearned for people to gain inspiration from this version of King, rather than what he deemed to be a watered-down myth. Jackson's was the only overt

DOI: 10.1057/9781137589149.0007

interpretation of the site inconsistent with the view of the Memorial as universal and inclusive. But while other speakers offered abstract and unifying interpretations of the Memorial, most turned to partisan and divisive remarks at some point in their speeches. These speakers risked alienating audience members with their other less universal and more political remembrances of King.

Politicization

Many speakers took the Memorial's dedication as an opportunity to discuss a host of political issues. Several dedicators advanced their own political positions under the guise of what King would want/think/say/do, including Bernice King, who repeated she could "hear [her] father," and Young, who proclaimed, "That's what Dr. Martin Luther King would have you do!"[18] Even speakers who did not explicitly cite King's retrofitted opinions on contemporary issues still appropriated his words to make political arguments. Yet after many speakers cultivated a political memory of King, Obama retreated back to the universal memory, recrafting and using that public memory to enhance his own personal ethos. In this section, I examine how Obama and the other dedicatory speakers cultivated and used the public memory of King for their own purposes.

The conduit of justice

A number of speakers adopted language from a quotation on the nearby inscription wall: "Injustice everywhere is a threat to justice everywhere." These speakers used the quotation, imbued with universal values, to make unequivocally political points. Far from the dedicators' broad interpretations of the Memorial and its goals, many speakers used the language of "justice" and "injustice" to cultivate a partisan and usable memory of King.

In her opening remarks, Ifill first brought up the theme of "injustice" saying, "It would be easier to dwell on the adversity, the indignities, the injustice, but then perhaps we would give short shrift to the inspiration that arose from every challenge we face." She called instead for speakers to "celebrate the dream."[19] Ironically, the very next speaker, Gray, instead chose to focus on "the yolk of injustice" and added that the "dream remains unfulfilled." Gray framed the issue of District of Columbia

DOI: 10.1057/9781137589149.0007

residents' lack of representation in Congress under the language of injustice. Gray called the nation's capital the "last remaining battlefront of the American Revolution" and said, "In 1966, Dr. King marched in our streets calling for an end to this injustice."[20] But while King did take a stance on this particular issue during his lifetime, other speakers associated King's call for justice with issues that originated, more or less, after King's death.

Martin Luther King III focused on justice, rather than injustice, wrapping his entire message around the theme and linking his father's memory to the still-new Occupy Wall Street movement. He said, "The young people of the Occupy Movement all over this country and throughout the world are seeking justice." Assuming a sermonic tone he continued,

> Justice for the unemployed searching for months for jobs... Justice for working class people barely making it. Justice for middle class folks who are unable to pay their mortgages. Justice for elders terrified that they are losing the value of their savings and their healthcare. Justice for the young people who graduate from college [and] are unemployed and burdened by student loans they cannot repay. Justice for everyone who are simply asking the wealthy and corporations to pay their fair share....We must stand up for social and economic justice.[21]

King III's decision to tie his father's memory to the Occupy movement was timely and controversial. The Occupy movement, which launched in September of that year, featured demonstrators protesting various issues of perceived economic injustice. The movement gained significant media coverage and helped lead *TIME Magazine* to name "The Protester" as its Person of the Year. But movement participants were also vilified as radicals and criticized for lacking clear goals.[22] King III only linked the general goals of the Occupy movement with those of his father, but others more closely linked King's memory to the movement.

Bernice King was one such speaker, who again used the "justice" language of her father saying, "Perhaps the postponement [of the dedication ceremony] was a divine interruption to remind us of the King that moved us beyond the dream of racial injustice to the action and work of economic justice." As she continued, Bernice King quoted her father and also adopted language of the Occupy movement. She said,

> Perhaps God wanted to remind us that forty-three years ago... that [King] was in the midst of starting a poor people's campaign where he was galvanizing

DOI: 10.1057/9781137589149.0007

poor people from all walks of life to... *occupy* this place until there was change in the economic system and a better distribution of wealth. In fact over forty-three years ago [King] told us that we must become "maladjusted to certain social ills." We should never adjust to the one percent controlling more than 40% of the wealth. We should never adjust to an unprecedented number of people being unemployed.[23] (Italics mine)

By citing divine providence, Bernice King moved beyond her father's most famous address to make his memory germane to the Occupy movement. Furthermore, she combined King's words (e.g., "economic justice," "social ills") with those of the Occupy movement (e.g., "occupy," "the one percent") to create the impression that her father's beliefs were synonymous with those of the movement. Jackson went even further than Bernice King, opining, "Forty-three years after Dr. King planned an occupation on this same spot, he would say to the Occupiers of Wall Street... you are the children and offspring of Dr. King's Poor People's Campaign."[24] Jackson authorized members of the movement as the descendants and heirs of King's work. Moreover, Jackson (as one of King's fellow activists) and King's children (as his biological descendants) legitimized the Occupy movement's goals by tying them to King's supposedly universal value of "justice."

Sharpton connected King's memory to the Occupy movement and a laundry list of political issues by discussing the "fight for justice today." Sharpton ranted, "Justice is not trying to change the voting rights act and deny us in thirty-four states our right to vote with voter ID laws. Justice is not executing people on recanted testimonies. Justice is not sending children to schools that are not funded. Justice is not one percent of the country controlling 40% of the wealth."[25] Within the span of thirty seconds, Sharpton cited contentious voter ID laws enacted by Republican-controlled legislatures and the controversial execution of Troy Davis in September of that year, in addition to issues related to education and the economy.[26] Sharpton charged, "We will not stop until we get the equal justice Dr. King fought for," thereby linking King's vision of justice to the vision he described. More than anything, Sharpton saw King's memory as a tool for bringing up the issues for which he wanted to advocate. Sharpton outright said, "Dr. King was not just a historic figure, he was a conduit of a spirit of justice."[27] King as a "conduit," or instrument, or channel for a message of justice was more important to Sharpton (and seemingly for many of the other speakers) than King as a historical figure.

DOI: 10.1057/9781137589149.0007

At least two speakers refrained from speaking for King on any contemporary issues. Wright Edelmen discounted King's theoretical opinion on current issues, charging, "Dr. King is not coming back. We're it."[28] Bond seemed to agree when he described his experience talking to people about King:

> Since [King] died, a constant question I've received whenever a racial advance occurred was "What would Dr. King have said about this?" What would he say when America elected its first black president? Would he think that this achievement was a confirmation of his dream? Would he say that these things would not have happened if he had not lived? I've always felt he'd be pleased whenever any element of racial progress occurred. But he wouldn't think that Nirvana had come. And he wouldn't try to claim credit for everything.[29]

By abstaining from inventing positions for King to take on contemporary issues, Edelmen and Bond attempted to put questions of King's political positions to rest. But these speakers were in the minority, as others continued to treat King as a conduit of justice, employing his memory to make points on a litany of other issues including bullying, racial profiling, immigration reform, LGBTQ rights, and the corporatization of the news media.[30]

The president as King

For many speakers, the event was as much about Obama as it was about King. Nearly halfway through the event, Lowery was greeted with cheers when he humorously remarked, "We haven't got all day. I've got to go hear a fellow speak named Barack Obama."[31] Other speakers mentioned Obama's election as a "redemptive moment" (Jackson) and a "down payment" on King's Dream (Lewis).[32] In his own dedicatory remarks, Obama also spoke as much about himself as he did about King. Obama continued in the path of the other speakers by focusing on both the past and the present, insisting that "[o]ur work, Dr. King's work, is not yet complete."[33] Throughout the speech, Obama conflated "King's work" with "our work" and, moreover, *his own* work. Through an extended analogy linking himself to King, Obama cultivated and used a memory of King for the purpose of enhancing his own ethos. Importantly, in order to craft a memory useful for such a purpose, Obama retreated from the previous speakers' political remarks and offered rhetoric largely consistent with Condit's description of epideictic discourse as uncontroversial and universal.

DOI: 10.1057/9781137589149.0007

Through encouraging audience members to see past King's great speeches to his hard-fought actions, Obama also recalled an image of himself. For example, when describing the reasons for celebrating King's legacy, Obama offered, "It is right for us to celebrate Dr. King's marvelous oratory, but it is worth remembering that progress did not come from words alone. Progress was hard."[34] Similar to King, Obama had often been described as a skilled orator by both friends and foes. But to that point in his first term in office, Obama also faced critics who charged that the president was an effective speaker but not an effective leader. Therein, Obama responded to such critics, introducing oratory as "right... to celebrate," while also insisting that "progress was hard." Obama continued throughout the speech to relate himself to King as both a speaker and a leader. He said, "We forget now, but during his life, Dr. King wasn't always considered a unifying figure. Even after rising to prominence, even after winning the Nobel Peace Prize, Dr. King was vilified by many, denounced as a rabble rouser and an agitator, a communist and a radical." Obama may as well have been reciting his own biography, as the president, too, quickly rose to prominence, won the Nobel Peace Prize, and was vilified in nearly identical language. He continued, "[King] was even attacked by his own people, by those who felt he was going too fast or those who felt he was going too slow; by those who felt he shouldn't meddle in issues like the Vietnam War or the rights of union workers." Again Obama drew distinct parallels between his presidency and King's career, perhaps asking audience members to connect Obama's positions on labor rights and the wars in Iraq and Afghanistan to King's positions on issues such as class politics and the Vietnam War. Significantly, Obama took the comparison a step further, saying, "We know from his own testimony the doubts and the pain [King's decisions] caused him, and that the controversy that would swirl around his actions would last until the fateful day he died."[35] Obama's attribution of doubt and pain to King might have caused some audience members to see the same characteristics in the president. If audience members perceived Obama's and King's accomplishments as similar (as many already had), they might also identify the two as similar in their personal qualities.[36] Audience members, seeing Obama and King as alike, might also come to believe that Obama, although a polarizing figure at the time, might eventually come to be unifying and beloved as King.

DOI: 10.1057/9781137589149.0007

Alongside Obama's efforts to present himself as a unifying figure came the necessity of championing King's memory as unifying. The politically charged remembrances of King from other speakers might also make Obama into a political, rather than universal, figure. Therefore, Obama treaded lightly when speaking for King on a variety of issues and spoke in relatively uncontroversial terms. For instance, he said, "[King] tells us that we have a duty to fight against poverty, even if we are well off; to care about the child in the decrepit school even if our own children are doing fine; to show compassion toward the immigrant family, with the knowledge that most of us are only a few generations removed from similar hardships."[37] Importantly, Obama spoke for King on general ideas, rather than specific policies. Unlike other speakers, Obama eschewed endorsing the Occupy movement, avoided promoting policies, and refused to vilify his detractors.

In ways that further identified himself and King as unifying and reconciling figures, Obama adopted some of King's language and incorporated his own famous campaign vocabulary of "change."[38] He said, "[King] understood that to bring about true and lasting change, there must be the possibility of reconciliation; that any social movement has to channel this tension through the spirit of love and mutuality." By combining his words with those of King, Obama also linked their ideologies. He continued,

> And so on this day, in which we celebrate a man and a movement that did so much for this country, let us draw strength from those earlier struggles. First and foremost, let us remember that change has never been quick. Change has never been simple, or without controversy...Change requires determination.[39]

Obama encouraged audience members to see King's "change" from the civil rights movement as comparable to Obama's political vision of "change." Audience members, who saw Obama as similar to King and saw "change" as comparable to the outcome of the civil rights movement, might come to see "change" as inevitable and worth fighting for in spite of its slow, stubborn nature.

Clearly, Obama's notion of a politically solvent memory of King was very different from that of other speakers. For other speakers, the politicization of King's public memory meant adapting it to advocate positions on various controversial issues. For Obama, the politicization of the memory meant returning to the universal in an effort to promote himself and his own ideology as such.

DOI: 10.1057/9781137589149.0007

Institutionalization

As discussed in Chapter 3, the King Memorial's inclusion on the National Mall helped privilege and institutionalize the memory of King. In her dedicatory remarks, Bernice King explicitly discussed the institutionalization of King's memory as her mother's foremost goal, saying, "It was vitally important to [Coretta Scott King] that his life, words, and principles become institutionalized."[40] Through the remarks and performances of several dedicators, the commemorative ceremony also helped institutionalize King's memory as a chief part of the nation's hegemonic establishment.[41] In this section, I examine how event participants institutionalized King's memory as a part of a larger national narrative of progress and how they turned him from a vernacular voice into a hegemonic figure.

A chapter in the story

Many speakers commented on the Memorial's placement on the National Mall, advocating that the placement ultimately allowed King's memory to become a part of a larger national narrative of progress. Salazar advocated, "We have a duty to make sure that all of America's story is told, not just a part of it. And with the dedication of this Memorial, we are honoring a critical chapter in America's story."[42] Honored with a Memorial on the "front yard of America" (Lewis), King's story became its own chapter in the nation's larger narrative; one situated alongside chapters about presidents and war heroes.[43] Christine King Farris, especially excited about her brother's placement next to specific presidents, exclaimed, "I am overjoyed and humbled to see this great day, when my brother Martin takes his symbolic place on the National Mall near America's greatest presidents including Abraham Lincoln, Thomas Jefferson, and Franklin Roosevelt."[44] Obama pointed out the noteworthiness of King's placement near such figures, reminding audience members that King, a black preacher never elected to office, now stood among monuments to soldiers and the nation's political leaders. Obama justified King's placement, adding, "[King] gave voice to our deepest dreams and our most lasting ideals... [and] stirred our conscience and thereby helped make our union more perfect."[45] For Obama, King's story belonged on the Mall because like the stories of various presidents and wars, his story concerned the perfection of the union and progress of the nation.

DOI: 10.1057/9781137589149.0007

Thus, also for Obama, King concurrently fit in and stood out among the surrounding monuments. As someone who helped make the "union more perfect," King's goals and overall effect on the nation could be judged as comparable to those of the other icons memorialized on the Mall. As an African American social activist, King also remained unique. Consistent in theme but unique in detail, King's story fit as a chapter in "America's story" as narrated by the National Mall.

Surely the entirety of "America's story" is impossible to tell, at least within the confines of the National Mall. Indeed, only select stories of certain wars, presidents, and other figures and events are depicted on the landscape. Additionally, the King Memorial does not come close to recounting the entire story of the civil rights movement. Obama clarified the Memorial's meaning beyond its included inscriptions and physical components saying, "[T]his memorial is not for [King] alone. The movement of which he was a part depended on an entire generation of leaders." He named Rosa Parks, Dorothy Height, Benjamin Hooks, Fred Shuttlesworth, and the "multitudes of men and women whose names never appear in history books," declaring, "To those men and women, to those foot soldiers for justice, know that this monument is yours, as well."[46] But even accepting the Memorial as synecdochical for such people still omits major figures and events of the "story."

Remarks by Obama, Salazar, and others positioning King as an important figure in "America's Story," did more than privilege and institutionalize King's memory. With their remarks the speakers also seized King from his place as a vernacular leader and placed him alongside Lincoln and Jefferson as a national hero. Indeed, Lowery proudly declared, "[King] has become a father of the country."[47] But King's memory made the transition from vernacular to hegemonic in other ways at the dedication ceremony, as well.

From vernacular to hegemonic

Gwen Ifill introduced Jackson, Lewis, and Young as individuals who "walked beside Dr. King and have lived his legacy in the years since."[48] While this group of speakers did not talk about institutionalizing King's memory, they symbolically helped in the process because they had each, more or less, made the actual transition from being vernacular voices to being members of the establishment themselves. Jackson, who described

DOI: 10.1057/9781137589149.0007

himself as a "disciple" of King, unsuccessfully ran for the presidency and helped his son campaign in a successful bid for a seat in the House of Representatives.[49] Lewis, who recounted his experience marching with King on the National Mall, transitioned from social activism to a long term in the House of Representatives. Finally, Young, who had supported King as a member of the Southern Christian Leadership Conference, also served as mayor of Atlanta, Georgia, a Congressman, and US ambassador to the United Nations. Lewis remarked on his own journey and the state of the nation, saying, "I hear too many people saying that 48 years later that nothing has changed. Come and walk in my shoes; Dr. King is telling you that we have changed. That we are better people. We're a better nation."[50] Lewis, now an empowered and privileged part of the American government by virtue of his elected position as a US Congressman, defended the nation and its people against criticism from the vernacular. Lewis, Jackson, and Young all represented ways in which the official institutions of the US government were carrying on King's legacy. As the living remnants and stewards of King's legacy, their privileged positions in society helped the establishment adopt the public memory of King.

Event participants consummated the process of institutionalizing the Memorial's privileged memories of King and the civil rights movement immediately following Obama's address. The president linked arms with First Lady Michelle Obama, Vice President Joe Biden, Second Lady Jill Biden, and others for a rendition of the famous civil rights anthem "We Shall Overcome." The song, led by a large racially diverse choir, saw the entire crowd link arms, sway from side to side, and sing,

> We shall overcome,
> We shall overcome,
> We shall overcome some day
> Oh, deep in my heart
> I do believe
> We shall overcome some day.[51]

The sight of an African American president singing the song at the dedication may have also signaled to some that "some day" was today and that the nation had indeed "overcome." In spite of the many issues laid out by the president and other speakers, the late appearance of the hopeful song may have led some to believe that the real work was behind them. Ultimately, the president singing the song at a national event of commemoration helped transform the song from a civil rights anthem

DOI: 10.1057/9781137589149.0007

into an institutionalized national anthem and further transformed King from a voice of protest into an institutionalized national icon.

Conclusion and implications

This chapter yields several conclusions and implications. First, the interpretations of the site offered by event speakers primarily demonstrate the plurality of meanings available to observers. While a majority of the speakers agreed for the most part in their broad interpretations, Jackson's more unique interpretation of the sculpture's posture reveals one alternative reading. Additionally, Obama's insistence that the Memorial also commemorates individuals such as Rosa Parks and Fred Shuttlesworth gives credence to the idea that visitors may project their own meanings onto the site, even when those meanings are not physically included in the Memorial itself. Depending on prior knowledge and expectations, visitors may interpret the Memorial as inclusive of a wide range of people, places, events, and ideas. The more universal interpretations offered of the site, for instance as a Memorial "for the world," also encourage individuals to project their own meanings onto the Memorial, an opportunity many of the speakers took advantage of when offering their more political renderings of King's memory.

The most obvious finding is that dedicators cultivated and used partisan, present-focused public memories of King and the civil rights movement. Many public memory scholars offer similar conclusions, noting the uses of the past to address contemporary exigencies. Perhaps more unique to this case study are the number and variety of political causes advanced under the name of King. Immigration, voting rights, LGBTQ rights, financial reform, and the corporatized media are only some of the issues overtly mentioned by the event's speakers. Perhaps the promoted memory of King as a national or universal hero allowed speakers to appropriate his memory in attending to such a range of issues. The Memorial and its dedicatory speakers, presenting King's generic ideals as transcendent and his selected words as not needing context, allowed speakers to appropriate King's words and even to invent King's thoughts on issues as they pleased.

On a related note, in previous chapters I have mentioned the "ownership" of King's memory. The issue certainly arose in the dedication ceremony, as speakers claimed knowledge of King's views often by virtue

DOI: 10.1057/9781137589149.0007

of their relationship to King (e.g., son, sister, daughter, disciple, fellow marcher, or admirer). But perhaps Obama's identification with King, along with his place as the most privileged speaker at the event, made him the interpreter, inheritor, and owner-in-chief. As Shawn Parry-Giles and Trevor Parry-Giles assert, "no other individual possesses authority and power to influence collective memory more than the President of the United States."[52] The authors' assertion is bolstered in this case by the ways others linked the two together throughout Obama's presidency and by the ways Obama identified with King in his own address.

Obama and others were able to claim "ownership" of King's memory and politicize it in certain ways without much contestation, in part because of the exclusive lineup of event participants. The lack of ethnic, racial, and political diversity among dedicators allowed for a one-sided political forum and also detracted from the professed vision of the Memorial as inclusive, universal, and belonging to the world. The lack of certain voices also allowed the event to go by without mention of any perceived flaws in the Memorial's various visual and textual components.

Additionally, the dedication ceremony advanced and supplemented the institutionalization of King's memory. The presence of activists-turned-elected officials, such as Lewis and Young, along with the first African American president symbolically and actually represented a shift from the vernacular to the hegemonic. The discussion of King's story as a chapter in a larger American narrative also institutionalized King and portions of the civil rights movement. Yet as the speakers canonized King's memory as a chapter in "America's Story," they neglected to publish some of the details. While the event participants sang the uplifting "We Shall Overcome," recalled famous lines from King's works, and named prominent civil rights leaders, they left unsung other anthems and poems, ignored certain speeches and writings, and excluded the names of more controversial movement leaders. The actual history of the civil rights movement was often omitted in favor of certain memories

Notes

1   Michael E. Ruane and Michelle Boorstein, "Earthquake Alters MLK Plans," *Washington Post* (August 24, 2011), http://www.washingtonpost.com/blogs/

DOI: 10.1057/9781137589149.0007

post_now/post/earthquake-alters-mlk-plans/2011/08/24/gIQAHWIvbJ_blog.
html.

2   Barack Obama, dedicatory remarks in *Martin Luther King Memorial Dedication*,
    C-SPAN video and transcript, 3:22:36, Martin Luther King Jr. National
    Memorial, October 16, 2011, http://www.c-spanvideo.org/program/302020-1.

3   Balthrop, Blair, and Michel, "The Presence of the Present," 171.

4   Christine King Farris, dedicatory remarks in *Martin Luther King Memorial
    Dedication*, *C-SPAN* video, 3:22:36, Martin Luther King Jr. National Memorial,
    October 16, 2011, http://www.c-spanvideo.org/program/302020-1.

5   Harry Johnson, dedicatory remarks in *Martin Luther King Memorial
    Dedication*, *C-SPAN* video, 3:22:36, Martin Luther King Jr. National Memorial,
    October 16, 2011, http://www.c-spanvideo.org/program/302020-1.

6   By overt interpretations, I mean direct comments about understanding the
    Memorial's features, goals, and accomplishments.

7   Other speakers and performers included the Reverend Doctor Joe Samuel
    Ratliff; Mary Mary singers Erica and Trecina Atkins-Campbell; Poet Nikki
    Giovanni; General Motors chairman and CEO Dan Akerson; founder of
    the Tommy Hilfiger Corporation Tommy Hilfiger; Foundation Executive
    Leadership Council Co-Chairman Gary Cowger; violinist Miri Ben-Ari; Poem-
    Cee performers Black Picasso and DJ Stylus; actor Cicely Tyson; twelve-year-old
    actor Amandla Stenberg; actor/singer Diahann Carroll; Secretary-Treasurer
    of the American Federation of State, County, and Municipal Employees Lee
    Saunders; Alpha Phi Alpha Fraternity general president Herman "Skip" Mason;
    singer Aretha Franklin; and singer and pianist Stevie Wonder.

8   Bernice King, dedicatory remarks in *Martin Luther King Memorial Dedication*,
    C-SPAN video, 3:22:36, Martin Luther King Jr. National Memorial, October
    16, 2011, http://www.c-spanvideo.org/program/302020-1.

9   Julian Bond, dedicatory remarks in *Martin Luther King Memorial Dedication*,
    C-SPAN video, 3:22:36, Martin Luther King Jr. National Memorial, October
    16, 2011, http://www.c-spanvideo.org/program/302020-1.

10 I do not mean to depreciate Ben-Ari's role as a performer; I only want to
    draw attention to the conspicuous absence of non-American speakers.

11 The only possible exceptions to this statement include Ben-Ari (who played
    the violin and did not speak) and the corporate sponsors (e.g., Akerson and
    Cowger) whose political persuasions were kept personal.

12 As I discuss in the next section, the lack of political diversity also allowed
    political remarks to go uncontested from conservative viewpoints at the event.

13 Joseph Lowery, dedicatory remarks in *Martin Luther King Memorial
    Dedication*, *C-SPAN* video, 3:22:36, Martin Luther King Jr. National Memorial,
    October 16, 2011, http://www.c-spanvideo.org/program/302020-1.

14 B. King, dedicatory remarks in *Martin Luther King Memorial Dedication*.

DOI: 10.1057/9781137589149.0007

15   Al Sharpton, dedicatory remarks in *Martin Luther King Memorial Dedication*, *C-SPAN* video, 3:22:36, Martin Luther King Jr. National Memorial, October 16, 2011, http://www.c-spanvideo.org/program/302020–1.

16   Obama, dedicatory remarks in *Martin Luther King Memorial Dedication*.

17   Jesse Jackson, dedicatory remarks in *Martin Luther King Memorial Dedication*, *C-SPAN* video, 3:22:36, Martin Luther King Jr. National Memorial, October 16, 2011, http://www.c-spanvideo.org/program/302020–1.

18   B. King, dedicatory remarks in *Martin Luther King Memorial Dedication*; and Andrew Young, dedicatory remarks in *Martin Luther King Memorial Dedication*, *C-SPAN* video, 3:22:36, Martin Luther King Jr. National Memorial, October 16, 2011, http://www.c-spanvideo.org/program/302020–1.

19   Gwen Ifill, dedicatory remarks in *Martin Luther King Memorial Dedication*, *C-SPAN* video, 3:22:36, Martin Luther King Jr. National Memorial, October 16, 2011, http://www.c-spanvideo.org/program/302020–1.

20   Vincent Gray, dedicatory remarks in *Martin Luther King Memorial Dedication*, *C-SPAN* video, 3:22:36, Martin Luther King Jr. National Memorial, October 16, 2011, http://www.c-spanvideo.org/program/302020–1.

21   Martin Luther King III, dedicatory remarks in *Martin Luther King Memorial Dedication*, *C-SPAN* video, 3:22:36, Martin Luther King Jr. National Memorial, October 16, 2011, http://www.c-spanvideo.org/program/302020–1. Cheryl Wharry discusses the distinct features of African American sermonic discourse, including "rhyme, tempo, pitch, and formulaic language." Cheryl Wharry, "Amen and Hallelujah Preaching: Discourse Functions in African American Sermons," *Language in Society* 32, no. 2 (2003): 204. See also, Geneva Smitherman, *Talkin and Testifyin: The Language of Black America* (Boston: Houghton Miffin, 1986).

22   Andrew Ross Sorkin, "Occupy Wall Street: A Frenzy That Fizzled," *New York Times* (September 17, 2012), http://dealbook.nytimes.com/2012/09/17/occupy-wall-street-a-frenzy-that-fizzled/. The Arab Spring and other protests throughout the world also influenced *TIME*'s Person of the Year decision.

23   B. King, dedicatory remarks in *Martin Luther King Memorial Dedication*.

24   Jackson, dedicatory remarks in *Martin Luther King Memorial Dedication*.

25   Sharpton, dedicatory remarks in *Martin Luther King Memorial Dedication*.

26   For further background on controversies surrounding voter ID Laws and Troy Davis, see Pam Fessler, "The Politics Behind New Voter ID Laws," *NPR. org* (July 18, 2011), http://www.npr.org/2011/07/18/138160440/the-politics-behind-new-voter-id-laws; and CNN Wire Staff, "Troy Davis Put to Death in Georgia," *CNN Justice* (September 22, 2011), http://www.cnn.com/2011/09/21/justice/georgia-execution/index.html.

27   Sharpton, dedicatory remarks in *Martin Luther King Memorial Dedication*.

28   Marian Wright Edelmen, dedicatory remarks in *Martin Luther King Memorial Dedication*, *C-SPAN* video, 3:22:36, Martin Luther King Jr. National Memorial, October 16, 2011, http://www.c-spanvideo.org/program/302020–1.

DOI: 10.1057/9781137589149.0007

29 Bond, dedicatory remarks in *Martin Luther King Memorial Dedication.*
30 Bernice King commented on several of these issues in rapid-fire fashion, saying, "We should never adjust to violence of any form, bullying or being bullied. We should never adjust to policies and practices that profile people because of their color, their ethnicity, or their nation of origin." Martin Luther King III linked his father to a position on LGBTQ rights, describing him as "a champion of human rights and social justice for all people regardless of race, gender, sexual orientation or nationality." Finally, Dan Rather spoke on the "corporatization, the politicization and the trivialization of the news." See B. King, dedicatory remarks in *Martin Luther King Memorial Dedication*; King III, dedicatory remarks in *Martin Luther King Memorial Dedication*; and Dan Rather, dedicatory remarks in *Martin Luther King Memorial Dedication*, *C-SPAN* video, 3:22:36, Martin Luther King Jr. National Memorial, October 16, 2011, http://www.c-spanvideo.org/program/302020-1.
31 Lowery, dedicatory remarks in *Martin Luther King Memorial Dedication.*
32 Jackson, dedicatory remarks in *Martin Luther King Memorial Dedication*; and John Lewis, dedicatory remarks in *Martin Luther King Memorial Dedication*, *C-SPAN* video, 3:22:36, Martin Luther King Jr. National Memorial, October 16, 2011, http://www.c-spanvideo.org/program/302020-1.
33 Obama, dedicatory remarks in *Martin Luther King Memorial Dedication.*
34 Ibid.
35 Ibid.
36 For examples of articles comparing Obama to King, see Lara Seligman, "Obama's Close Ties to Martin Luther King Jr.," *National Journal* (August 11, 2011), http://www.nationaljournal.com/mlk/obama-s-close-ties-to-martin-luther-king-jr--20110811; and "King and Obama: Eleven Things in Common," *BET News* (August 23, 2011), http://www.bet.com/news/national/photos/2011/08/king-and-obama-11-things-in-common.html#!081011-news-national-martin-luther-king-barack-obama-1.
37 Obama, dedicatory remarks in *Martin Luther King Memorial Dedication.*
38 Although a broad and abstract word, I would argue that "change" carries specific connotations when used by Obama since he built his 2008 presidential campaign around the themes/words of "change" and "hope." I assert that these terms are also ideographs, defined by Michael Calvin McGee as "the basic structural elements, the building blocks of ideology." Heather Stassen and Benjamin Bates add, "although the terms appear vague at the surface, members of a community will be able to understand the ideograph's exact nuances and subtleties as understood within that community." By using the ideograph of "change," Obama links his ideology to King's. Michael Calvin McGee, "The 'Ideograph': A Link Between Rhetoric and Ideology," *Quarterly Journal of Speech* 66 (1980): 7; and Heather Stassen and Benjamin Bates, "Constructing Marriage: Exploring Marriage as an Ideograph," *Qualitative Research Reports in Communication* 11, no. 1 (2010): 1.

DOI: 10.1057/9781137589149.0007

39   Obama, dedicatory remarks in *Martin Luther King Memorial Dedication*.
40   B. King, dedicatory remarks in *Martin Luther King Memorial Dedication*.
41   By "hegemonic establishment" and "institution," I refer to the official customs, laws, stories, and organizations of the US government. However, in other cases, churches, media outlets, nonprofits, and other organizations can also be considered institutional and/or hegemonic.
42   Ken Salazar, dedicatory remarks in *Martin Luther King Memorial Dedication*, *C-SPAN* video, 3:22:36, Martin Luther King Jr. National Memorial, October 16, 2011, http://www.c-spanvideo.org/program/302020-1.
43   Lewis, dedicatory remarks in *Martin Luther King Memorial Dedication*.
44   King Farris, dedicatory remarks in *Martin Luther King Memorial Dedication*.
45   Obama, dedicatory remarks in *Martin Luther King Memorial Dedication*.
46   Obama, dedicatory remarks in *Martin Luther King Memorial Dedication*. Briefly, Rosa Parks, Dorothy Height, Benjamin Hooks, and Fred Shuttlesworth are some of the most often publicly remembered activists of the civil rights movement. They are also notable here as each had passed away within the six-year period prior to the speech. Shuttlesworth's death had come most recently, only days before the event on October 5, 2011. See E. R. Shipp, "Rosa Parks, 92, Founding Symbol of Civil Rights Movement, Dies," *New York Times* (October 25, 2005), http://www.nytimes. com/2005/10/25/us/25parks.html?pagewanted=all; Margalit Fox, "Dorothy Height, Largely Unsung Giant of the Civil Rights Era, Dies at 98," *New York Times* (April 20, 2010), http://www.nytimes.com/2010/04/21/us/21height. html; Emma Brown, "Former NAACP Leader Benjamin L. Hooks Dies at 85," *Washington Post* (April 16, 2010), http://www.washingtonpost.com/ wp-dyn/content/article/2010/04/15/AR2010041505771.html; and Jon Nordheimer, "Rev. Fred L. Shuttlesworth, and Elder Statesman for Civil Rights, Dies at 89," *New York Times* (October 5, 2011), http://www.nytimes. com/2011/10/06/us/rev-fred-l-shuttlesworth-civil-rights-leader-dies-at-89. html?pagewanted=all&_r=0.
47   Lewis, dedicatory remarks in *Martin Luther King Memorial Dedication*.
48   Ifill, dedicatory remarks in *Martin Luther King Memorial Dedication*.
49   Jackson, dedicatory remarks in *Martin Luther King Memorial Dedication*.
50   Lewis, dedicatory remarks in *Martin Luther King Memorial Dedication*.
51   Dedication Choir, performance in *Martin Luther King Memorial Dedication*, *C-SPAN* video, 3:22:36, Martin Luther King Jr. National Memorial, October 16, 2011, http://www.c-spanvideo.org/program/302020-1.
52   Shawn J. Parry-Giles and Trevor Parry-Giles, "Collective Memory, Political Nostalgia, and the Rhetorical Presidency: Bill Clinton's Commemoration of the March on Washington, August 28, 1998," *Quarterly Journal of Speech* 86, no. 4 (2000): 419.

DOI: 10.1057/9781137589149.0007

5
Conclusion

Abstract: *Chapter 5 concludes the book, drawing from and expanding on the discussions in each chapter in order to offer a robust and inclusive assessment of the Memorial. In the chapter, I offer specific implications related to the contested "ownership" of King's memory, its placement in an institutional narrative of progress, and its problematic universalization.*

Keywords: King Memorial; multivocal rhetoric; Owning King's Memory; public memory; Vernacular to Hegemonic

Walker, Jefferson. *King Returns to Washington: Explorations of Memory, Rhetoric, and Politics in the Martin Luther King, Jr. National Memorial.* New York: Palgrave Macmillan, 2016. DOI: 10.1057/9781137589149.0008.

Situated in the interdisciplinary field of public memory studies, this book attended to the memory of Martin Luther King Jr. as cultivated by the King National Memorial, its surrounding landscape, and many of its supplementary texts. While other scholars have observed the memory of King and the civil rights movement, this study made new contributions by concentrating on King's memory as constructed at the national level by entities such as the National Parks Service and the president of the United States. Furthermore, as scholars, activists, educators, and members of the media continue to mourn the lack of depth of knowledge of King's life and the glossing over of his ideals, this study's robust approach significantly enriched the field of scholarship concerned with King's public memory.

Throughout this study, I have argued that the King Memorial helps construct and institutionalize the public memory of King in concurrently universal, inclusive, political, and partisan ways, ultimately becoming a contentious site of remembrance. I sought answers to questions such as the following: How do the Memorial's various components add contour to King's public memory? How might the site's visitors, critics, and producers arrive at different, sometimes conflicting interpretations of the site? How do related discursive texts influence the Memorial's cultivation of King's public memory? Furthermore, I specifically contended that the Memorial and its related texts support different claims to "ownership" of King's memory. I argued that the site reconciles the memory of King and the civil rights movement with a "mainstream" national narrative of progress, institutionalizing King and turning him from a vernacular voice into a hegemonic figure. Finally, I advanced the case that the Memorial and its related discourse universalize King's memory, turning the site into a contentious and contested rhetorical battlefield. I conclude my analysis in the following chapter by, first, reviewing the results of each preceding chapter, in turn recapitulating the answers to my research inquiries. Second, I return to my larger contentions to offer further implications on King's public memory and the overall field of memory studies. Third, I discuss the study's limitations and suggest future directions for related research.

Study results

I utilized a multifaceted approach throughout this study, acknowledging that rhetorical memory sites and, indeed, all rhetorical artifacts support

DOI: 10.1057/9781137589149.0008

multiple meanings and interpretations. Understanding rhetoric as "multivocal," my analysis sought to account for many potential readings of the King Memorial.[1] Moreover, I also heeded Victoria Sanchez and Mary Stuckey's assertion that "[m]any…texts contain both hegemonic and emancipatory messages, with considerable tensions created between them."[2] Throughout this study, I sought to uncover such tensions inherent in the King Memorial and its surrounding and supporting texts. Before discussing the total results and implications of the study, it is beneficial to review the findings of each chapter.

Chapter 2 recounted the history of the King Memorial, discussing issues related to its origins, location, design, and funding. While the project took many years to launch, the professed goals of the Memorial's original producers (e.g., various members of Congress and Alpha Phi Alpha Fraternity) were consistently universal in theme. However, the selection of the Memorial's location and design caused conflict among the project's various creators and observers. Disputes over the Memorial's proximity to the Lincoln Memorial, the employment of a Chinese sculptor and use of Chinese granite, and the inclusion of a paraphrased quotation were some of the issues that complicated the collaborative process of building the Memorial and led to tensions in the site's final form. Additionally, fundraising issues caused some people to question the motives of Alpha Phi Alpha Fraternity, the King family, and various corporations for their perceived attempts to "own" King's memory. Chapter 2 served multiple purposes by unveiling conflicts related to the Memorial, while also amassing privileged and vernacular interpretations of the site.

Based primarily on my own visits to the King Memorial, Chapter 3 offered a rhetorical analysis of the site's textual composition, visual design, and surrounding landscape. I tendered a multivalent reading of the site consistent with Blair, Jeppeson, and Pucci's insistence on locating the "multiple, frequently conflicting messages" of a memory site.[3] I also incorporated Dickinson, Ott, and Aoki's concept of the experiential landscape, observing how the physical and cognitive surroundings of the King Memorial might influence how visitors interpret the site.[4] The King Memorial's decontextualized inscriptions, abstract visual metaphor, and placement on the National Mall help construct and institutionalize a public memory of King as a national/universal hero. But while the Memorial enables universal and positive interpretations, the site's layout, the King statue's physical appearance, and the existence and subsequent

DOI: 10.1057/9781137589149.0008

removal of a controversially paraphrased quotation also allow for more awkward and pessimistic readings of the Memorial. Meanwhile, the site's many omissions encourage visitors to forget some of King's actual positions and actions, as well as other prominent strands and leaders of the civil rights movement. Also significantly, Barack Obama's presence in the site's physical and cognitive landscapes links the president to King's memory. Through each of these observations, I argued that the Memorial places more emphasis on the present than the past and does more to inspire than to educate.

Chapter 4 examined the King Memorial's dedication ceremony as supplementary rhetoric that has the potential to influence how visitors interpret the site. The analysis revealed that, while many of the speakers' most overt interpretations presented the Memorial as unifying and inspiring, they also cultivated partisan memories of King, tying his legacy to various contemporary political causes. Rather than linking King to modern-day issues, Obama connected King's ideology and biography to his own, thus cultivating a memory of the icon that could serve to enhance his own ethos. Obama and other speakers also helped institutionalize King's memory by noting the Memorial's placement on the National Mall and King's own placement among other national heroes such as Abraham Lincoln and Thomas Jefferson. Furthermore, by situating King's memory as part of a national narrative of progress and by featuring speakers that transitioned from outsider/activists to insider/ elected officials, the dedication ceremony also helped King transition from a vernacular voice to a hegemonic leader in public memory. The three-pronged focus of Chapter 4 on the interpretation, politicization, and institutionalization of King's memory enriches an understanding of how the King Memorial functions.

This study's multifaceted approach attended to critical, popular, and official interpretations of the King Memorial. Explicating and analyzing these interpretations has led to many implications concerning the public memory of King and public memory studies in general. While each chapter made cogent arguments and offered their own answers to my research questions, a combined reading of these analyses leads to larger results and implications. Herein, I return to my larger arguments, drawing from the results of each chapter to offer a fuller discussion of King's public memory as cultivated by the King Memorial and its related texts. First, I discuss the implications of the argument that the Memorial and its related texts support different claims to the "ownership" of King's memory.

DOI: 10.1057/9781137589149.0008

Claims of ownership

Over one year after the King Memorial opened to the public, the January 21, 2013, edition of *The Daily Show with Jon Stewart* featured a segment on the coinciding celebrations of Obama's second inaugural and MLK Day. The segment asked, "What Dr. Martin Luther King Jr. Would Have Wanted" and presented commentary by gun rights, pro-life, and Occupy Wall Street activists claiming that King would have agreed with their respective positions. Gun Appreciation Day organizer Larry Ward said, "I believe that Gun Appreciation Day honors the legacy of Dr. King... The truth is I think Martin Luther King would agree with me if he were alive today." "Senior Black Correspondent" Larry Wilmore responded by pleading for people to stop invoking King in political arguments, saying "Dr. King is dead... so you don't get to use him as your imaginary black 'yes man.'"[5]

The segment humorously brought forth the issue of politicizing and even "owning" King's memory. This study has demonstrated the ways in which various individuals cultivated a political memory of King, linking him to a host of positions on major and contentious political issues. To prevent King from becoming the "imaginary black 'yes man,'" I echo Balthrop, Blair, and Michel's call for a distinction "between legitimate appropriation and irresponsible exploitation of the past for present 'use.'"[6]

Perhaps more significant than the use of King's memory are the varied claims to its ownership. Throughout the process of imagining, designing, raising funds for, and building the King Memorial, many individuals and groups claimed King's memory for their own. For example, some African Americans, such as artist Gilbert Young, responded harshly to the use of a Chinese sculptor on the project by asserting, "King is ours."[7] Others such as Alpha Phi Alpha responded by asserting that King belonged to the entire world, but then also claimed ownership for themselves in many ways by promoting its members to leadership positions on the project throughout its completion, sometimes being criticized for mishandling King's memory. The King family, who literally owns the rights to many of King's words, was also criticized throughout the Memorial's completion for dishonoring King's memory. Meanwhile, a fundraising campaign saw large corporations donate to the project and, in a sense, own part of the Memorial. Such instances saw critics rail against the Memorial's use of corporate dollars and question whether King would be happy with the Memorial at all.[8] The Memorial's dedication ceremony speakers also made some claims to memory ownership by virtue of their relationship to

DOI: 10.1057/9781137589149.0008

King (e.g., disciple, son, daughter, and follower). These ethos-enhancing moves helped various speakers in their previously described efforts to use King's memory for their partisan agendas.

Given the nation's sordid history of slavery and King's legacy of fighting against racial inequality, any efforts (intentional or otherwise) to treat his memory as chattel, or property, are troubling. Additionally, while many rhetors appropriated King's memory in efforts to recast King in political contexts, the Memorial's bookstore and fundraising efforts, in Kent Ono and Derek Buescher's sentiments, "made it possible to recast the figure...within a western, capitalist frame."[9] In other words, fundraising efforts allowed patrons to own a piece of the King Memorial, while the bookstore encourages visitors to own pieces of King. King's image and words are commodified and sold through posters, postcards, books, films, magnets, and other products. In consideration of King's positions on issues of economic justice, this type of ownership and transformation of his memory is also problematic.

Chief among those claiming ownership of King's memory was Obama, who identified with King throughout his dedication address and also served, as rhetoricians Shawn Parry-Giles and Trevor Parry-Giles would note, as the "chief interpreter of public memory."[10] Obama's own claims to authority over King's memory were made possible by the Memorial and its surrounding experiential landscape. Although the Memorial's universal themes inherent in its design and text supplement the idea that the Memorial belongs to all of humankind, the site subtly endorses Obama as the principle inheritor and owner of King's memory. The cognitive landscape of the Memorial links Obama to King in many ways, as visitors might recall media discussions of Obama as the fulfillment of King's "dream."[11] Obama's physical presence at the Memorial (on the shelves of the bookstore and at the dedication ceremony) and in its surrounding physical landscape (at the White House or elsewhere in Washington) further privilege Obama's connection to King. Obama helped recast King's memory in both political and capitalist frames through his oration and through his appearance on items at the bookstore. But Obama also helped recast King's memory in another significant way: from vernacular voice to hegemonic leader.

From vernacular to hegemonic

Obama's claim to ownership over King's memory, coupled with his position as president, enabled him to institutionalize King's memory in many

DOI: 10.1057/9781137589149.0008

ways. Furthermore, the Memorial's placement on the National Mall and its universalization of King's ideals also transform King from a vernacular presence to a part of a hegemonic national narrative of progress.

I discussed the Memorial's placement on the National Mall in Chapters 2 and 3. For the Memorial's producers, conflict over deciding where to place the Memorial on the National Mall was as heated as any discussion over its design or inscriptions. In many ways, the placement of the Memorial seemed as important as its other features (if not more so). The eventual location adjacent to the Franklin Delano Roosevelt Memorial and in a supposed "line of leadership" with the Lincoln and Jefferson Memorials was highlighted by the Memorial's producers on their website, in brochures, and in other supplementary texts. As I discussed in Chapter 3, the site's location places King's memory next to those of its surrounding figures. Situating King next to Jefferson and Lincoln compares not only the three individuals but also their ideals (e.g., equality and freedom) and works (e.g., "I Have a Dream," the Declaration of Independence, and the Gettysburg Address). The Memorial's grand design and immediately surrounding physical landscape (e.g., the cherry blossom and American elm trees) also allow the King Memorial to fit in on the National Mall and thus to fit in with the other figures memorialized there.

As discussed in Chapter 4, Obama and other speakers commented on the Memorial's placement in their dedicatory remarks. Moreover, they treated the National Mall as a landscape that tells "America's story" and discussed the King Memorial as reciting a chapter of that story. Placing King's story in an official national narrative further compared his goals, accomplishments, and ideals to those of other national icons, including George Washington, Lincoln, and Roosevelt. Such comparisons are significant because of the ways King differed from these men. Whereas they were white presidents who rose through the ranks in the military or political realm, King was an African American social activist and preacher who was never elected to a federal office. While the placement next to presidential memorials is more often noted, the King Memorial is also located near monuments to war.[12] Again, the differences between King and war veterans are more pronounced than their similarities. King, an activist who practiced and preached nonviolence and stood up to national injustices, now stands next to veterans who physically fought in war contexts on the nation's behalf. But as King is now compared to presidents, so too is he deemed comparable to soldiers of the nation's wars. The commonality between the presidents, soldiers, and King, in Obama's words, was that they all "helped make our union more perfect."[13]

The King Memorial then tells the story of the betterment of the nation, as do the other memorials around it. Within the national story, King serves as a central leader much like Washington or a World War II hero. The civil rights movement then functions as a necessary event to move the nation forward, much like the Civil War, the New Deal, or World War II. The National Mall's memorials explain that Lincoln had to lead the nation through the Civil War in order to end slavery and reunite the nation; that Roosevelt and the nation had to suffer through the Great Depression and World War II in order to attain greater peace and prosperity; and that King and his fellow activists had to endure the trials of the civil rights movement in order to advance racial equality. The telling of King's story by Obama, as both King's heir apparent and president, and by figures such as John Lewis, who made the literal transition from activist/outsider to elected official/insider, served to turn King's memory from vernacular to hegemonic. The Memorial's placement on the National Mall cemented that turn, placing King's memory in the hegemonic landscape of America.

Potential positive implications from King's shift to hegemonic are many. As Lewis remarked in his dedicatory address, "I hear too many people saying that 48 years later that nothing has changed. Come and walk in my shoes, Dr. King is telling you that we have changed. That we are better people. We're a better nation."[14] Marking and institutionalizing changes in racial equality and other areas is significant and worthwhile. Additionally, institutionalizing King's philosophy of nonviolence is also considerably important. But more negative consequences are also possible. For example, while the Memorial legitimizes the strategy of nonviolence, it also seems to justify the strategy of war. To be sure, the King Memorial displays an inscription denouncing the Vietnam War, and the site's dedication ceremony saw some people invent antiwar positions for King in regard to the ongoing conflicts in Iraq and Afghanistan.[15] However, by standing among numerous war memorials on the National Mall and by being placed alongside war heroes in the national narrative, the King Memorial suggests that strategies of nonviolence and war are compatible and equally legitimate.

Additionally, King's placement next to truly hegemonic figures in America's past may serve to silence some of his criticisms about the

DOI: 10.1057/9781137589149.0008

nation's government, instead of legitimizing all of his views. The statue's depiction as silent and still, and the site's inscriptions, devoid of context and packed with universal themes, fail to introduce many points of criticism by King that may be unresolved. Still, as the Lincoln Memorial has long stood as a site where Lincoln's memory has been reappropriated by vernacular voices (such as King's), the King Memorial may now have the potential for similar use. Thus King's memory, even transformed from vernacular to hegemonic, may still be of use to various activists. The site's potential usefulness to the hegemonic and vernacular introduces this study's final implication concerning the Memorial as a contentious and contested battleground.

The contentious and contested

Throughout this study, I have demonstrated the contentious and contested dynamics of the King Memorial. This observation is interesting and, perhaps, perplexing in consideration of the site's universal themes inherent in its visual and textual features and in the words of its producers and dedicators. Still, the Memorial has been contentious throughout its history.

As I thoroughly observed in Chapter 2, the Memorial's origins saw conflict and compromise over its location and design. Organizations argued over the Memorial's location, each with a different idea of where King would fit best symbolically on the National Mall. While the Memorial's design easily gained approval from the same organizations, the selection of a Chinese sculptor and the eventual design of King's statue drew heavy criticism from other individuals and groups. Finally, the most heavily covered disagreement concerned the inclusion of the paraphrased "Drum Major" quotation. That controversy resulted in the eventual removal of the quotation, demonstrating the impact that supplemental or critical rhetoric can have on a site of memory. All of these conflicts arose in spite of the project's organizers' publicly professed motives of creating a unifying Memorial with universal appeal.

In Chapter 3, I discussed how the Memorial also creates conflict through the familiar dialect of remembering and forgetting. While the remembering/forgetting pairing is, as Blair, Dickinson, and Ott say, "an assumptive cliché in public memory studies," the omission of historical context from the Memorial allows for conflict over interpreting the

DOI: 10.1057/9781137589149.0008

Memorial's meaning.[16] Whereas Philip Wander's concept of the "Third Persona," indicates that rhetoric "negate[s] through silence," Blair, Dickinson, and Ott recognize that memory sites cannot be all inclusive and that public memory is constituted by the whole of a memory field, rather than one site or artifact. But I add that the omission of details still makes a difference, as visitors come to memory sites with different knowledge and expectations. For example, I noted Obama's projection of figures such as Rosa Parks and Fred Shuttlesworth onto the site in Chapter 4. Yet individuals with less knowledge of the civil rights movement might not connect those figures to the site, as they are not mentioned by name on its walls. Others might project figures including Malcolm X onto the Memorial's walls, while more still might come only with limited knowledge of King's "Dream" speech at hand. The lack of context for understanding enables conflicting interpretations of the Memorial.

Similarly, the Memorial's included inscriptions are fragmented from larger texts and stripped of context in order to "seem more important than the whole from which [they] came."[17] Aside from the conclusion that the Memorial's pedagogical functions fall by the wayside to the site's inspirational goals, this observation again demonstrates the site's creation of conflict in its efforts to promote the universal. Most obviously, the paraphrased "Drum Major" quotation, arrogant rather than abstract, fails in its aim to be read as universal. But as I observed in Chapter 4, even the most universal quotations (e.g., "Justice anywhere…") may be used for different partisan purposes. Again, the quotations imbued with universal values but stripped of their context enable wildly different interpretations.

As demonstrated through the differing interpretations presented in Chapters 2 and 4 by the site's dedicators and critics, and as noted in my own analysis of the site in Chapter 3, the King Memorial encourages conflicting interpretations. I submit that the King Memorial's insistence on the universal is actually the driving force behind the contentious and competing readings. The Memorial's concentration on the universal endeavors to cultivate a memory of King as, in historian Vincent Gordon Harding's words, "the convenient hero."[18] The Memorial's cultivation of the universal hero or national savior does not quell historians' concerns over the loss of understanding of who King actually was, but it does allow for claims of ownership over his memory. Thus, I come full circle with my analysis. The cultivation of a universal memory of King also

DOI: 10.1057/9781137589149.0008

allows for his memory to be owned and used for a variety of partisan and political purposes. Ultimately, the universal leads the King Memorial to its place as a contentious and contested battlefield.

Limitations and areas of future research

While this book has made significant contributions to understanding public memory and the specific memory of Martin Luther King Jr., this study is also limited in many ways and leaves open a variety of paths for future research.

Notably, this study examined King's public memory as cultivated by a national memorial and its related texts. Although I offered a multifaceted approach, I could not possibly include analyses of each text related to the monument. Articles of criticism, speeches of praise, and other fragments of the site remain available for rhetorical analysis. Additionally, further research could take a more focused approach through an in-depth analysis of discourse I did study. For example, employing a different lens to examine Obama's dedicatory address might reveal more about how the president used King's memory to his political advantage. Other scholars might be interested in other artifacts and events that I briefly mentioned throughout the study, such as Glenn Beck's 2010 rally at the Lincoln Memorial and the Rocky Mount City Memorial to King, that might be worthy of rhetorical analysis in their own right.

While I briefly discussed Gallagher's research on Atlanta's national remembrance of King, another interesting study might compare and contrast the two sites. Similarly, additional studies might compare the King Memorial with other King or civil rights-related museums and monuments throughout the country. Other comparative analyses could examine the King Memorial and its dedication ceremony with another memorial from the National Mall and its corresponding dedication. Such a study might yield deeper understanding of the differences and similarities in commemorating a nonelected, nonviolent activist and a president or a war hero.

I have already mentioned the potential usefulness of theoretically differentiating the use from the misuse of public memory. Much work can be done toward that cause for scholars interested in the idea. However, this book invites other approaches from memory studies scholars, as well. I discussed remembering and forgetting throughout the

DOI: 10.1057/9781137589149.0008

study, but did not dwell on the potential positive implications of the King Memorial's omissions. Perhaps future research might follow memory scholar Bradford Vivian's lead in examining forgetting as a "form of negation," but also potentially "a productive and even desirable aspect of collective life, ethics, and decision making."[19] In the main, I have also combined the approaches of memory scholars, most notably including Balthrop, Blair, and Michel and Dickinson, Ott, and Aoki.[20] By examining the visual and textual components of a memory site, its surrounding experiential landscape, its historical-contextual background, and various supplementary and/or critical discourse, I have provided a template for a fuller approach to studying a memory site. This approach is especially useful for multivocal readings of sites where scholars wish to amass various interpretations. Some critics might attempt this approach for memorials that seem difficult to interpret, as recovering the apparent motives of its creators and the readings of critics or privileged interpreters might enable a better understanding.

Conclusion

Throughout this book, I have analyzed the King Memorial and its supporting texts' cultivation of the public memory of Martin Luther King Jr. I have discussed the ways in which the Memorial's various components and related texts affect King's public memory and how various individuals arrive at different kinds of readings of the site. I argued that the site supports various claims to "ownership" of King's memory, that it institutionalizes King as a hegemonic figure in a national narrative, and that it creates contention through the universalization of certain of King's ideals.

The issues discussed throughout this book have continued to present themselves since the opening and dedication of the King Memorial in 2011. King's memory continues to be institutionalized and universalized, most notably in recent years by President Obama. At his second inaugural, Obama further identified with King and helped institutionalize his memory by taking the oath of office on both King's and Lincoln's Bibles.[21] Again, Obama linked King's legacy to his own and to Lincoln's, continuing to situate King as a figure in official national memory. Two months later, Obama laid a small stone from the King Memorial on the grave of Yitzhak Rabin, an Israeli prime minister assassinated for his efforts to make peace with the Palestinians.[22] In addition to Obama using King's memory once again, this act also continued to promote King's memory as unifying, universal, and relevant to the entire world.

The King Memorial itself continues to be a contentious site of memory. While celebrating MLK Day in 2013, people continued to engage in debate over the paraphrased quotation that had not yet been removed and the King sculpture's image.[23] In March 2013, an apparent rift developed between the Martin Luther King Jr. National Memorial Project Foundation and members of the King family. The organization responsible for the King Memorial was forced to drop King's name from their title, becoming known only as the Memorial Foundation.[24]

As familiar issues reappear, rhetorical critics must diligently investigate the potential promise and problems associated with the cultivation of King's public memory. So too must activists and teachers take note. King's works and words alike hold valuable lessons. Herein, advocates for those lessons find a call to teach, to inform, to resculpt memory, and to reassert the importance of history.

Notes

1   Blair, Jeppeson, and Pucci, "Public Memorializing in Postmodernity," 264.
2   Sanchez and Stuckey, "Coming of Age as Culture?" 78.
3   Blair, Jeppeson, and Pucci, "Public Memorializing in Postmodernity," 269.
4   Dickinson, Ott, and Aoki, "Spaces of Remembering and Forgetting," 31.
5   "What Dr. Martin Luther King Jr. Would Have Wanted," *The Daily Show with John Stewart*, featuring John Stewart and Larry Wilmore (January 21, 2013), http://www.thedailyshow.com/watch/mon-january-21-2013/what-dr--martin-luther-king-jr--would-have-wanted.
6   Balthrop, Blair, and Michel, "The Presence of the Present," 196.
7   See Fulbright, "State NAACP Joins Protest of Chinese Artist Chosen for MLK Monument."
8   See Watkins, "Five Questions Dr. King Might Ask."
9   Ono and Buescher, "*Deciphering Pocahontas*," 25.
10 Parry-Giles and Parry-Giles, "Collective Memory, Political Nostalgia, and the Rhetorical Presidency," 420.
11 For example, see "Most Blacks Say MLK's Vision Fulfilled, Poll Finds."
12 Again, the Memorial's website and supplementary pamphlets made more of the site's position in a "line of leadership" with the Jefferson and Lincoln Memorials. Meanwhile, speakers at the site's dedication also talked more often about the site's placement near presidential memorials.

DOI: 10.1057/9781137589149.0008

13   Obama, dedicatory remarks in *Martin Luther King Memorial Dedication*.

14   Lewis, dedicatory remarks in *Martin Luther King Memorial Dedication*.

15   See King III, dedicatory remarks in *Martin Luther King Memorial Dedication*; and Jackson, dedicatory remarks in *Martin Luther King Memorial Dedication*.

16   Blair, Dickinson, and Ott, "Introduction," 18.

17   McGee, "Text, Context, and the Fragmentation of Contemporary Culture," 280.

18   Harding, "Beyond Amnesia," 468.

19   Bradford Vivian, "On the Language of Forgetting," *Quarterly Journal of Speech* 95, no. 1 (2009): 90.

20   See Balthrop, Blair, and Michel, "The Presence of the Present;" Dickinson, Ott, and Aoki, "Memory and Myth at the Buffalo Bill Museum;" and Dickinson, Ott, and Aoki, "Spaces of Remembering and Forgetting."

21   Paige Lavender, "Obama Inauguration Bible: President, John Roberts Inscribe Traveling King Family Bible," *Huffington Post* (January 21, 2013), accessed March 28, 2013, http://www.huffingtonpost.com/2013/01/21/obama-inauguration-bible_n_2523130.html.

22   Ian Johnston, "Obama Lays Stone from MLK Memorial on Grave of Israeli PM Slain for Trying to Make Peace," *NBC News* (March 22, 2013), accessed March 28, 2013, http://worldnews.nbcnews.com/_news/2013/03/22/17413043-obama-lays-stone-from-mlk-memorial-on-grave-of-israeli-pm-slain-for-trying-to-make-peace?lite.

23   Hampton Dellinger, "Righting Two Martin Luther King Memorial Wrongs," *The Atlantic* (January 21, 2013), accessed March 28, 2013, http://www.theatlantic.com/politics/archive/2013/01/righting-two-martin-luther-king-memorial-wrongs/266944/.

24   Melanie Eversley, "Dispute Between King Family, Memorial Foundation Denied," *USA Today* (March 27, 2013), accessed March 28, 2013, http://www.usatoday.com/story/news/nation/2013/03/27/king-foundation-family/2026545/.

DOI: 10.1057/9781137589149.0008

Index

DOI: 10.1057/9781137589149.0009

DOI: 10.1057/9781137589149.0009

Lightning Source UK Ltd.
Milton Keynes UK
UKOW02n1009121215

3617UKLV00003B/8/P